I0426294

Point Transect Sampling for Monitoring Passerine Birds in Denali National Park and Preserve

An Assessment of 2002-2008 Pilot Data

Natural Resource Technical Report NPS/CAKN/NRTR—2012/589

Steven T. Hoekman, Mark S. Lindberg

Institute of Arctic Biology
University of Alaska
Fairbanks, AK, 99775

June 2012

U.S. Department of the Interior
National Park Service
Natural Resource Stewardship and Science
Fort Collins, Colorado

The National Park Service, Natural Resource Stewardship and Science office in Fort Collins, Colorado publishes a range of reports that address natural resource topics of interest and applicability to a broad audience in the National Park Service and others in natural resource management, including scientists, conservation and environmental constituencies, and the public.

The Natural Resource Technical Report Series is used to disseminate results of scientific studies in the physical, biological, and social sciences for both the advancement of science and the achievement of the National Park Service mission. The series provides contributors with a forum for displaying comprehensive data that are often deleted from journals because of page limitations.

All manuscripts in the series receive the appropriate level of peer review to ensure that the information is scientifically credible, technically accurate, appropriately written for the intended audience, and designed and published in a professional manner. Data in this report were collected and analyzed using methods based on established, peer-reviewed protocols and were analyzed and interpreted within the guidelines of the protocols.

Views, statements, findings, conclusions, recommendations, and data in this report do not necessarily reflect views and policies of the National Park Service, U.S. Department of the Interior. Mention of trade names or commercial products does not constitute endorsement or recommendation for use by the U.S. Government.

This report is available from the Natural Resource Publications Management website (http://www.nature.nps.gov/publications/nrpm/).

Please cite this publication as:

NPS 184/114759. June 2012

Contents

Contents (continued)

Figures

Figures (continued)

Tables

Executive Summary

Passerine birds (passerines) in Denali National Park and Preserve (Denali) have been selected for long-term monitoring as part of the National Park Service's (NPS) Inventory and Monitoring Program. Monitoring goals include relating bird distributions to habitat characteristics and detecting severe population declines over 20 years. Point transect surveys were implemented to monitor breeding passerines because distance sampling methods adjust counts for probability of detection, require only 1 visit to each sampling point during a breeding season, and allow monitoring of multiple species because males are easily identified by their songs. Our objectives were to analyze pilot data to 1) assess adherence to assumptions of distance sampling, 2) examine factors influencing detection probabilities, 3) estimate density across years and habitats, and 4) examine statistical power to detect future population declines.

Sampling was conducted during June 2002-2008 at a systematic grid of locations in Denali north of the Alaska Range. At each grid location, point transects were centered on 25 sampling points separated by 500 m. Using standard point transect methods, observers enumerated and estimated distance to all passerines detected during a 10 minute interval. During 2002-2008, 35 separate grid locations were sampled, with some sampled in up to 5 years. Twenty three observers surveyed 1,331 point transects, with 12,623 detections of 80 species. Of 14 species with sufficient samples for analyses, we found that all 5 species of thrushes as well as Arctic Warblers, Fox Sparrows, and Dark-eyed Juncos (see Table 4 for scientific names) showed a relative surplus of detections at intermediate distances (~40-70 m). This pattern likely arose from bird evasion of observers and/or error in distance estimation. Resulting violations of critical assumptions of distance sampling were uncorrectable; hence, these species were unsuitable for distance sampling analyses.

Estimated detection functions for 6 remaining species adequately met assumptions when data were pooled across years. However, we found large variation in detection functions relative to year, habitat type, and wind speed. Resulting functions often severely violated assumptions of methods, were biologically implausible, and were inconsistent across species and with our predictions. We also found consistent differences in detection functions relative to individual observers. Observers often had surpluses or deficits of observations at specific distances, most likely as a result of error and bias in distance estimates to birds detected only by auditory cues. We concluded estimates of detection probability and hence density were likely subject to large bias and variability. Furthermore, we failed to identify satisfactory remedies and felt density estimates from these data would be uninformative. Even if we ignored potential bias in year-specific estimates, power analyses suggested current methods and levels of sampling effort would be unlikely to meet the monitoring goal of >80% power to detect a 50% population decline over 20 years for multiple species.

We concluded that characteristics of Denali made distance sampling methods inappropriate for monitoring populations of passerines and that impediments would be difficult or impossible to overcome. Instead, we recommended survey methods allowing estimation of probability of detection that do not rely on estimation of distance to birds and that will be relatively insensitive to evasive movements by birds.

Acknowledgments

We are indebted to personnel from the National Park Service (S. Andersen, R. Drum, M. Knoche, J. Mizel, M. Paulson, and J. Wells) and Alaska Bird Observatory (P. Elstner, C. Erwin, K. Hannah, E. Miller, L. Tauzer, T. Walker) who collected data used in these analyses. We would also like to thank M. MacCluskie, C. L. McIntyre, and J. H. Schmidt for helpful discussion and comments.

Photo credit: National Park Service

Introduction

The Vital Signs program implemented by the Central Alaska Network (CAKN) seeks to monitor ecosystem change and responses of biota (MacCluskie and Oakley 2005). Birds often serve as useful indicators of ecological condition because of their high position in most food webs (Fancy and Sauer 2000, O'Connell et al. 2000). During the breeding season, many male birds can be identified by their songs, and multiple species may be sampled using standardized surveys (Sauer et al. 2003). Passerines comprise the majority of the bird species in the CAKN and are monitored as part of the NPS Inventory and Monitoring Program. Goals for monitoring passerines at Denali included relating distributions to habitat characteristics and having 80% power to detect a 50% decline in populations over 20 years for multiple species.

Large-scale programs to monitor passerines commonly have utilized point counts, which enumerate birds detected from a sampling location during brief sampling interval. Point count methods do not account for probability of detection and thus provide an index to population size (Nichols et al. 2009). If detection probability does not change meaningfully through time and its variation is relatively small, point count methods can provide a useful assessment of population trends (Johnson 2008). Extensive standardization of sampling protocols has sought to minimize heterogeneity in detection probability (Peterjohn 1994, Ralph et al. 1995). However, numerous studies have documented large variation in detection relative to factors such as observer, time of day, time of season, year, and climatic conditions (Robbins 1981, Skirvin 1981, Link and Sauer 1998, Farnsworth et al. 2002, Norvell et al. 2003, Sauer et al. 2003, Bibby et al. 2007). Because heterogeneity in detection can bias density estimators, estimation of probability of detection is recommended (Rosenstock et al. 2002, Nichols et al. 2009). Point transects use distance sampling methods to estimate probability of detection relative to distance from the observer and are appealing because they typically require only 1 visit to each site, can be used for multiple species, and are robust to heterogeneity in detection (Buckland et al. 2001).

During 2002-2008, a pilot study using point transect surveys for breeding passerines was conducted in Denali to develop a standardized sampling protocol, obtain baseline information on abundance and distribution, and collect pilot data for evaluation of methods. Our objective was to assess whether implemented sampling and analytic methods would be sufficient to meet monitoring objectives. We partitioned this assessment into consecutive steps. We first assessed if assumptions of distance sampling were adequately met. Because modeling sources of variation in detection probability is integral to estimating density, we examined effects of year, observer, habitat type, and wind. Our penultimate goal was to estimate baseline densities for each species and variation in density relative to habitat type and year. However, we did not present these estimates because of evidence of substantial error and bias arising from violations of assumptions. Finally, we estimated statistical power of pilot methods to detect future population declines. We divided text after *Field Methods* into 2 sections. In Section I, we presented exploratory analyses relative to adherence to assumptions and variation in detection probability. In Section II, we addressed power to detect trends.

Methods

Study Area

Denali is located in central Alaska (63° 35.8'N, 149° 38.2'W) and is dominated by the Alaska Range (Fig. 1). Our study area roughly encompassed ~10,000 km^2 and 2 broad ecoregions in the northern foothills of the Alaska Range (Nowacki et al. 2002). Continental weather patterns prevail in the intermountane boreal region in the west, where the climate is relatively dry, seasonal temperature fluctuations are high, and fire is an integral disturbance process. The Alaska Range transitional region in the east shows intermediate conditions in the gradient toward maritime habitats characterized by wet climate, moderate temperature flux, and wind as a dominant disturbance process. Topography is generally rugged and mountainous, but broad glacial valleys and uplands intersperse the area (Fig. 2). Elevations ranged from ~500 to ~2,500 m. Common habitat types included lowland boreal forest and a variety of subalpine and alpine habitats (Paton and Pogson 1996). Vegetation communities included coniferous forest dominated by spruce (*Picea* spp.), shrub tundra dominated by birch (*Betula* spp.) and willow (*Salix* spp.), and high elevation tundra with herbaceous plants or barren rock.

Sampling Design

Sampling was based on a systematic grid of sampling locations with a random starting point separated by 20 km that was originally designed for monitoring vegetation (Roland et al. 2003). Within 10 km of the main park road and in selected areas of the Toklat basin, additional locations were placed 10 km from existing points (Fig. 1).

During 2002-2005, selection of locations for sampling was targeted to specific geographic areas during each year. Locations were selected to represent a wide range of habitats and elevations, and sampling effort was limited by available personnel. During 2004, the Rock Creek and Primrose locations were sampled 3 times to asses within season variation; these locations were selected in part because of ease of access. During 2006-2008, a serially alternating design with 3 panels of 8 locations was implemented. The pool of potential locations for this design was the 27 locations within 10 km of the main road. Of these, 24 were randomly selected and assigned to panels. Centered on each location, a grid of 25 points separated by 500 m defined centers for point transects.

Field Methods

Point transects

We used distance sampling methods (Buckland et al. 2001) to conduct point transect sampling of avian species. A crew of 2 located the sampling point and then waited for ~2 minutes for birds to resume normal behavior. For a 10 minute sampling period, the observer identified all birds, counted the number detected in each group (one or more birds of same species in close proximity, e.g. a pair or a flock), estimated the horizontal distance to each individual or flock, and noted the detection type (see below) for each group. The other crew member recorded data. Distances were estimated in 10 m intervals to 100 m, 25 m intervals from 100 to 150 m, and as >150 m. When approaching a transect, observers attempted to detect birds that flushed from near the transect center; these birds and their estimated distance from the center were recorded at the start of the sampling period. Based on the behavior and identities within each group, all of the following detection types that applied were recorded: 1) flying over area, 2) calling,

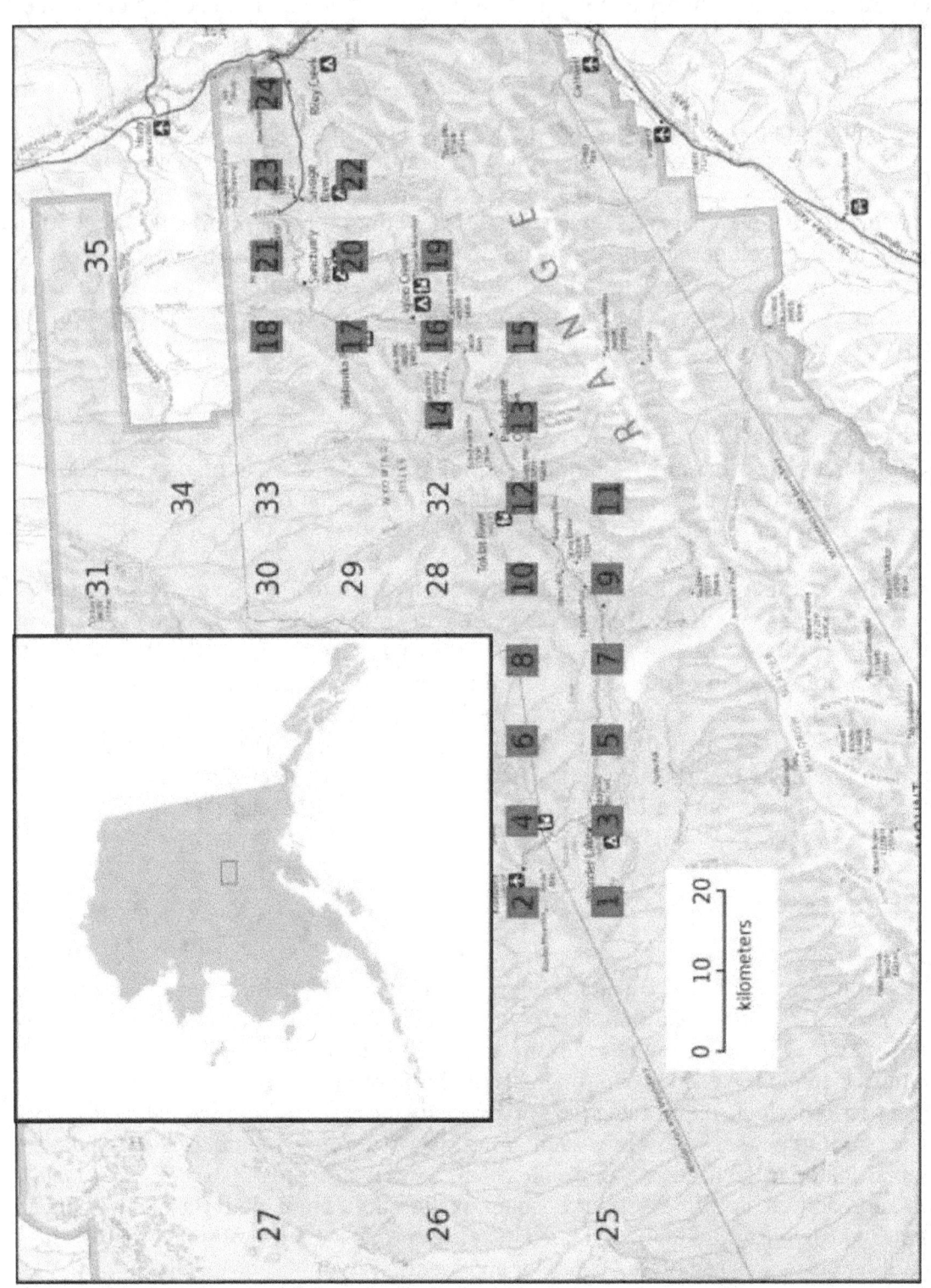

Figure 1. Sampling locations at Denali National Park and Preserve. Yellow locations were selected using targeted sampling; blue locations were included in the panel design selected from locations <10 km from the Denali Park road. Legend to site names on next page.

Label	Location	Latitude	Longitude
1	Muddy River	63.4371	-151.054
2	Reinhill	63.5260	-151.047
3	Wonder Lake	63.4329	-150.854
4	Upper Moose Creek	63.5224	-150.844
5	Lower Thorofare River	63.4286	-150.653
6	Moose Creek Canyon	63.5175	-150.645
7	Muldrow	63.4239	-150.453
8	Moose Creek N. Fork	63.5128	-150.444
9	Gorge Creek	63.4190	-150.252
10	Upper Stony Creek	63.5084	-150.241
11	Toklat West	63.4134	-150.054
12	Divide Mountain	63.5032	-150.040
13	Polychrome Pass	63.4977	-149.839
14	Tributary Creek	63.5852	-149.823
15	EFE	63.4915	-149.641
16	Igloo Creek	63.5813	-149.625
17	Middle Fork Teklanika River	63.6706	-149.612
18	Nika Ridge	63.7600	-149.598
19	Double Mountain	63.5753	-149.424
20	Sanctuary	63.6641	-149.412
21	Primrose Ridge	63.7539	-149.396
22	Upper Savage River	63.6583	-149.208
23	Mount Healy	63.7476	-149.193
24	Rock Creek	63.7410	-148.991
25	Hult Creek	63.4508	-151.860
26	Middle Birch Creek	63.6297	-151.844
27	Birch Bend	63.8087	-151.831
28	Lower Stony Creek	63.5978	-150.229
29	West Fork Toklat River	63.6872	-150.218
30	East Fork Toklat River	63.7765	-150.206
31	East Chitsia Mountain	63.9553	-150.183
32	Cabin Creek	63.8633	-150.094
33	Upper Widgand Creek	63.7713	-150.004
34	Lower East Fork Toklat River	63.8607	-149.991
35	Fish Creek	63.9326	-149.368

Sampling crew member on Primrose Ridge in Denali. Photo credit: National Park Service

Figure 1 (continued). Site names for locations sampled at Denali National Park and Preserve, 2002-2008

3) displaying, 4) ≥1 female, 5) ≥1 male, 6) singing, 7) pair (1 male and 1 female), 8) visual detection, and 9) detection of the same individual at the previous point transect. Crew members rotated between observer and recorder roles.

Covariate data

While at each point, the recorder also recorded the start time of sampling, temperature, and environmental conditions (Table 1), which were qualitative measures of conditions thought likely to influence detection probability. We characterized habitat at each sampling point using the level II classification of Viereck et al. (1992), which is based on species composition and physiognomy of existing vegetation (Table 2).

Figure 2. Steep, higher elevation terrain with scrub habitat near the Tributary Creek sampling location (A) and interspersed forest, scrub, and aquatic habitat on the valley floor near the Middle Birch Creek sampling location (B) in Denali. Photo credit: National Park Service

Table 1. Environmental conditions recorded by observers at each point transect immediately prior to sampling. Groupings describe the pooled categories that were used as covariates in models of detection functions. Percent occurrence is for each grouping relative to the total sample of point transects.

Attribute	Description	Grouping	% Occurrence
Wind	Calm Slight	Low	58
	Wind felt on face	Moderate	23
	Leaves in constant motion Raises dust; small branches move Small trees sway > 15 mph	High	19
Precipitation	None Fog or smoke	None	87
	Drizzle Showers Rain Sleet Light snow	Precipitation	13
Sky conditions	<10% cloud cover	Clear	25
	10-50% cloud cover 50-90% cloud cover	Partly cloudy	44
	>90% cloud cover	Overcast	32
Noise	No background noise	Low	33
	Barely reduces hearing	Moderate	36
	Noticeable reduction of hearing Prohibitive (greatly reduced hearing)	High	31
Insect disturbance	None Few present	Low	61
	Moderate	Moderate	24
	Heavy	High	15

Table 2. Level II habitat types of Viereck et al. (1992) at point transects for passerines in Denali, 2002-2008. Three habitat groupings were used to model effects of habitat on detection functions.

Level II	% Occurrence	Grouping	% Occurrence
Barren rock	9.5		
Bryoid herbaceous	0.5		
Graminoid herbaceous	2.7		
Forb Herbaceous	0.8	Open	46
Dwarf scrub	28		
Dwarf needle leaf	0.6		
Dwarf tree scrub	4.3		
Low scrub	32	Low scrub	32
Tall scrub	8.5		
Needle leaf forest	9.6	Forest	22
Mixed forest	3.5		
Broad leaf forest	0.2		

Section I: Exploratory Analysis

Statistical Analyses

Data Preparation and Exploration

Because including rapidly-moving individuals inflates density estimates, we censored observations of birds that were detected flying over the point transect area. We also excluded individuals detected at the previous transect, as these birds likely were fleeing in front of the observer. To limit our scope to species with potentially adequate samples for estimating trends in density and abundance, we considered only species with >200 observations. We used Program Distance (Thomas et al. 2009) to conduct standard distance sampling analyses of point transect data (Buckland et al. 2001, 2004). We conducted exploratory analyses to look for violations of assumptions of distance sampling, define appropriate data truncation, define appropriate groupings of detection distances for each species, and assess if similar species could benefit from pooling observations to estimate joint detection functions. For all analyses, we used Akaike's Information Criterion corrected for sample size (AIC_c) to select among competing models of detection function structure (Burnham and Anderson 2002). Because we wished to include effects of covariates on detection probability, we considered only key functions including a scale parameter. Unless otherwise stated, estimation of detection functions included choice among the following model structures: half-normal key function with either cosine or Hermite polynomial series expansions with ≤2 adjustment terms and hazard key function with either cosine or simple polynomial series expansions with ≤2 adjustment terms. For exploratory models of detection functions, we truncated observations at 250 m and used exact observation distances. To avoid observations with very low probability of detection, we right-truncated observations at distances where estimated probability of detection fell below ~0.15. Distance sampling assumes all groups near 0 distance are detected, detected groups are independent, groups do not move prior to detection, and distances are accurately estimated. To achieve robust estimates, detection functions should meet the shape criteria of being monotonically declining, asymptotically approaching 0, and having a relatively flat "shoulder," meaning that the slope of the detection function should be ~0 across the first 2 distance intervals. We grouped detections by distance into 6-8 intervals to meet shape criteria, and we favored applying the same or similar groupings and truncation points to facilitate comparison among species.

Estimating detection functions

Many of the measured covariates were likely to have some influence on detection functions. The ultimate goal of analyses was to understand and enhance our capacity to monitor trend in densities for multiple species across years. Making unbiased comparisons of inter-annual density requires modeling meaningful annual variation in detection functions. Therefore, our approach was to focus on modeling annual variation in detection functions and understanding factors most important to this variation. The 3 factors that we expected to be most influential to explaining annual variation were effects of individual observers, habitat type, and wind speed; our preliminary efforts were directed at understanding effects of these factors. Because detection will also depend on the behavior and characteristics of each species, we considered each species separately.

To assess support for inter-annual variation in detection functions, we created 3 different model structures that each represented a competing hypothesis about annual variation. The "pooled" model did not distinguish among years and represented the hypothesis of no meaningful annual variation. A "factor covariate" model allowed the key function and series expansion to be estimated separately for each year and represented the hypothesis that detection functions differed in both shape and scale across years. Finally, we considered a model that included year as a covariate that influenced the scale parameter of the key functions. This parameter controls the magnitude of detection probabilities, so this "scale covariate" model allowed detection functions across years to differ in scale but not shape. We selected a best approximating model using AIC_c. We used this model set and selection approach for all subsequent covariates.

Detection functions likely vary among observers as a result of differences in experience, hearing, estimation of distance, etc. (Emlen and DeJong 1992, Sauer et al. 1994, Simons et al. 2007). To assess variation in detection functions among observers within a species, we selected 3 observers with >1,500 observations and large overlap in years (2002-2005) and locations sampled. This approach yielded adequate samples (typically >75 for each observer-species combination) and reduced potential for confounding of effects related to species, locations (e.g., habitat, topography) and years (e.g., climatic conditions) with differences among observers. We pooled remaining observers in 1 category during model selection. Additionally, we hypothesized observers might differ consistently in the the detection process, and developed an omnibus test based on a χ^2 statistic to examine if individuals showed unique patterns of detection. To facilitate comparisons across species, we used the same 8 distance categories for American-tree Sparrows that were used for other species. Our null hypothesis was that the proportion of observations in each distance interval by individuals did not differ from proportions for all observers. For each observer-species combination, we generated predicted counts for each distance category by multiplying total observations for that combination by the proportion of observations in each distance category for all observers pooled. For each observer, we then summed the actual and predicted counts within each distance category across all species. Based on the observation that the sum of χ^2 random variables will also have a χ^2 distribution, we used a χ^2 statistic to test whether the 8 actual versus predicted counts for each distance category differed at a significance level of $\alpha=0.05$. The lack of complete independence between actual and predicted values had the effect of reducing their differences and hence the likelihood of rejecting the null hypothesis. Because these methods didn't require samples sufficient to estimate detection functions for each observer-species combination, we expanded analyses to include 3 additional observers that had large samples of observations in only 1 year (1 in 2005, 2 in 2007).

Habitat is also likely to strongly influence detection functions, as changes in composition and physiognomy of vegetation could alter sight lines and transmission of sound (Schieck 1997, Pacifici et al. 2008). Our strategy for examining effects of habitat was to create a small number of habitat groups from the more specific Level II classification of Viereck et al. (1992) so that each group would have sufficient samples of observations for estimation of detection functions for each species in each habitat group. Because most detections on point transects in our study depended our aural cues, we hypothesized increased vegetation density would reduce probability of detection at larger distances. Therefore, we defined 3 habitat groups based on a gradient from "open" (low, sparse vegetation) to "closed" (tall, dense vegetation) vegetation structure (Table 2; Fig 3a-c). Wind moving through vegetation can increase ambient sound and decrease probability of detection (Simons et al. 2007). Therefore, we predicted increased wind speed would alter detection functions by decreasing probability of detection at large distances. We did not include analyses considering >1 covariate because these models often failed to optimize (likely because of insufficient samples within factor levels or poor goodness-of-fit) and because extreme violations of shape criteria impeded interpretation models that did optimize.

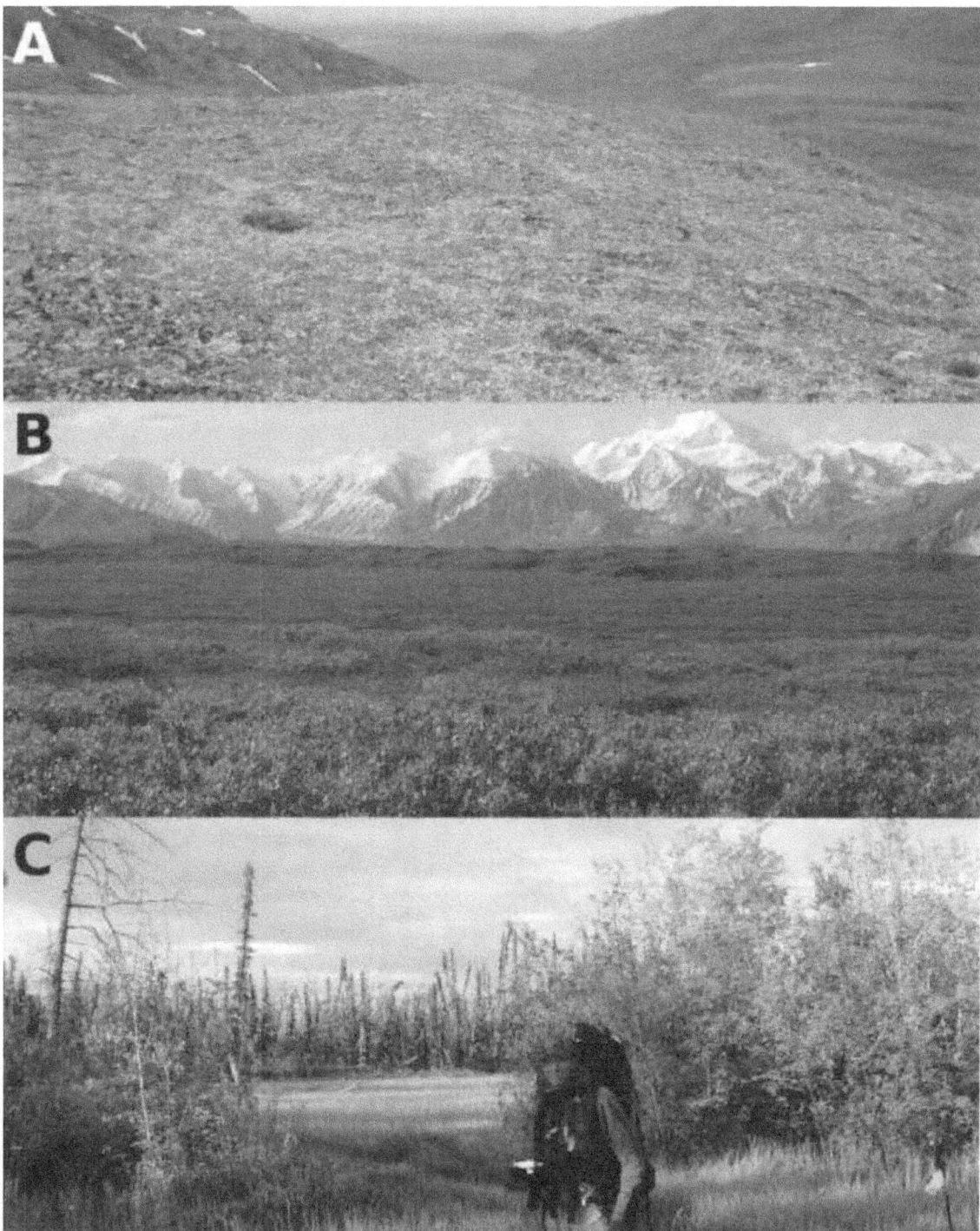

Figure 3. Examples of open (A; dwarf scrub), scrub (B; low scrub), and forest (C; mixed forest) habitat groupings used in analyses of detection probability during point transects for passerines in Denali. Photo credit: National Park Service.

Results

Sampling Effort

We sampled 35 different grids during June 2002-2008 (Table 3), with a mid-June peak in sampling (Fig. 4). Most grids were sampled once, but some were sampled in up to 5 years, resulting in a total of sample of 54 grid-year combinations. Sampling usually started after 03:00 h and finished before 09:00 h (Fig. 5) All 25 points were sampled at most grids, but some points were dropped because of flooding or presence of dangerous animals. In total, 1,331 point transects were sampled. A total of 23 observers detected 12,623 groups and 80 bird species, with >1,000 observations each year (Table 3). We censored 2 observations noted to have been located at the previous transect and 3.4% of observations that were of groups flying over the transect. Among remaining observations, 89% were detected while singing, 9% were detected while calling, and <4% were detected visually. In total, 98% of detections involved aural cues.

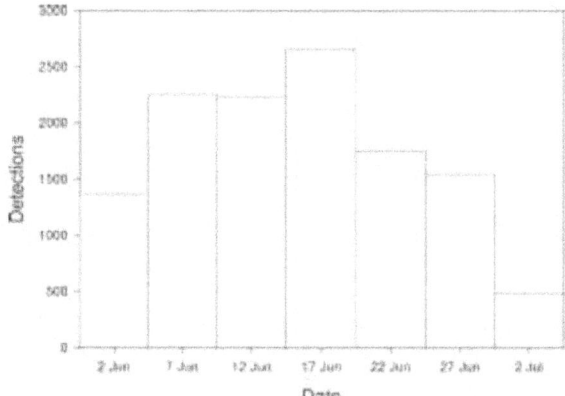

Figure 4. Frequency of detections of groups of passerines relative to date during point transects in Denali, 2002-2008.

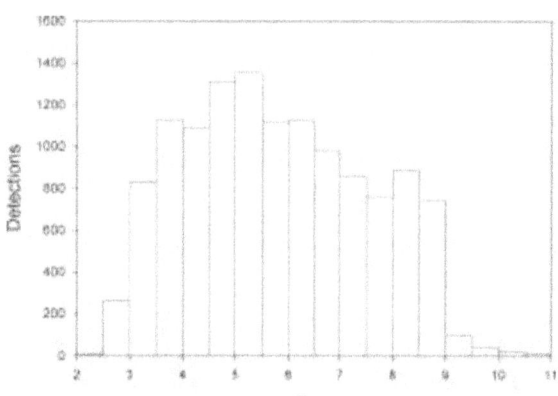

Figure 5. Frequency of detections of groups of passerines relative to hour of the day during point transects in Denali, 2002-2008.

Wilson's warbler (*Wilsonia pusilla*). Photo credit: Donna Dewhurst/USFWS

13

Table 3. Grids and point transects sampled and total number of observations during point transects in Denali, 2002-2008. Values indicate the number of out of 25 point transects that were sampled.

Grid	2002	2003	2004	2005	2006	2007	2008
Birch Bend				19			
Cabin Creek	11						
Divide Mountain						24	
Double Mountain							18
East Chitsia Mountain	20						
EFE							22
East Fork Toklat River	25						
Fish Creek		25					
Gorge Creek	13					16	
Hult Creek				23			
Igloo Creek				25	16		25
Lower Stony Creek	25						
Lower Thorofare River				25	25		
Lower East Fork Toklat River		25					
MCCN (Moose Creek Canyon)						25	
MCNF (Moose Creek N. Fork)							25
Middle Birch				25			
Middle Fork Teklanika River			25	25	25		
Mount Healy						25	
Muddy River							22
Muldrow				25	24		
Nika Ridge							25
Polychrome Pass				25	25		
Primrose Ridge	9	25	25[a]		25		
Reinhill						24	
Rock Creek			25[a]				25
Sanctuary						24	
Tributary Creek		20				24	
Toklat West							25
Upper Moose Creek				25	25		
Upper Savage River	19	25	24	24		25	
Upper Stony Creek					25		
Upper Widgand Creek		25					
West Fork Toklat River	25						
Wonder Lake				20	20		
Total mini-grids	8	6	4	11	9	8	8
Total points sampled	147	145	99[b]	261	210	187	187
Total Observations	1324	1459	1646	3541	1713	1846	1094

[a]Location sampled 3 times in 2004.
[b]194 point transects total, including points sampled >1 time.

Exploratory Analyses

Fourteen species had >200 observations (Table 4). Several sparrows and Wilson's warblers had >1,000 observations, but samples for most warblers and thrushes were much smaller. Exploratory models of detection functions using un-grouped distance intervals (Fig. 6a-c) revealed detection probability for most species fell below the minimum threshold of ~0.15 at distances >150 m, with the exception of some thrushes. Because the last distance category pooled all observations >150 m, it likely combined observations with a wide range of detection probabilities, some of which likely were <<0.15 even when the mean detection probability was >0.15. For this reason and to maintain consistency among species, we right-truncated all observations >150 m. Truncation resulted in substantial decreases in observations across species (overall reduction of 26%), but reductions were proportionally greatest for thrushes because of high frequencies of observations at longer distances.

Scaled relative frequencies of observations by distance (hereafter "scaled frequencies") showed some sparrows had sharply peaked frequency of detection near the transect center (Fig. 6a), suggesting attraction to observers (Thomas et al. 2010) and/or high detection probability at short distances. In contrast, most thrushes and some warblers showed maximum scaled frequencies at intermediate distances (Fig. 6b, c), which could result from birds near 0 distance hiding or from evasive movement of birds prior to detection. Fox sparrows and dark-eyed juncos showed spikes in scaled frequencies both near the transect center and at intermediate distances.

Table 4. Species with >200 observations during point transects in Denali, Alaska, 2002-2008.

Group	Species	Scientific name	n	truncated n
Sparrows and allies	White-crowned sparrow	Zonotrichia leucophrys	2,963	2,054
	American tree sparrow	Spizella arborea	1,227	937
	Savannah sparrow	Passerculus sandwichensis	1,206	1,097
	Fox sparrow	Passerella iliaca	1,218	664
	Dark-eyed junco	Junco hyemalis	502	455
Thrushes	Swainson's thrush	Catharus ustulatus	424	299
	Gray-cheeked thrush	Catharus minimus	263	202
	Hermit thrush	Catharus guttatus	296	130
	Varied thrush	Ixoreus naevius	208	130
	American robin	Turdus migratorius	225	129
Warblers	Wilson's warbler	Wilsonia pusilla	1,124	954
	Orange-crowned warbler	Vermivora celata	678	580
	Yellow-rumped (Myrtle) warbler	Dendroica coronata	239	227
Old world warblers	Arctic warbler	Phylloscopus borealis	270	165

Grouping observations into wider distance categories can improve detection functions by smoothing data and improving the function's "shoulder." This strategy can be effective if average evasive movement is <1/3 of the average detection distance, but grouping is ineffective if many birds near 0 distance are undetected (Buckland et al. 2001). Pooling observations for 4 thrushes and arctic warblers (Fig. 7) showed relatively few observations at <20 m and a peak at 50-60 m. These data suggest most birds initially near the transect center were either hiding or evading at least 40-60 m, which would be too large relative to the average detection distance (84 m) to be effectively remedied by grouping. Severe violations of assumptions made these species unsuitable for distance sampling analyses.

Spikes in scaled frequencies near the transect center also create difficulties for achieving a strong "shoulder" to detection functions. We sought to minimize this problem by grouping observations into wider intervals at short distances. This approach was adequate for white-crowned sparrows, where the relative spike in observations at 0-10 m was moderate. However, spikes in scaled frequencies both near the transect center and at intermediate distances for fox sparrows and dark-eyed juncos indicated multiple distribution problems, rendering these species unsuitable for distance sampling analyses. Small samples for hermit thrushes, especially near the transect center (e.g., 2 observations at 0-10 m), impeded reaching firm conclusions about the distribution of observations at small distances. However, a pattern of no overall decline in scaled frequencies from 20-150 m precluded estimation of a plausible detection function.

For remaining sparrows and warblers, we explored 3 different grouping schemes that we hypothesized would improve the "shoulder" of detection functions. We sought to create schemes with 6-8 distance intervals that had relatively even distribution of observations across intervals. We considered 7 groups with relatively even interval widths (cut points at 20/40/60/80/100/125 m) and 7 (30/50/70/90/100/125 m) or 8 (30/50/60/70/80/100/125 m) groups with wider intervals at small distances. We found the best distributions provided by 7 groups with even intervals for yellow-rumped warblers, 7 groups with wider intervals at small distances for American tree sparrow, and 8 groups with wider intervals at small distances for all other species.

Sampling crew member traveling on Sanctuary River in Denali.
Photo credit: Mark Paulson

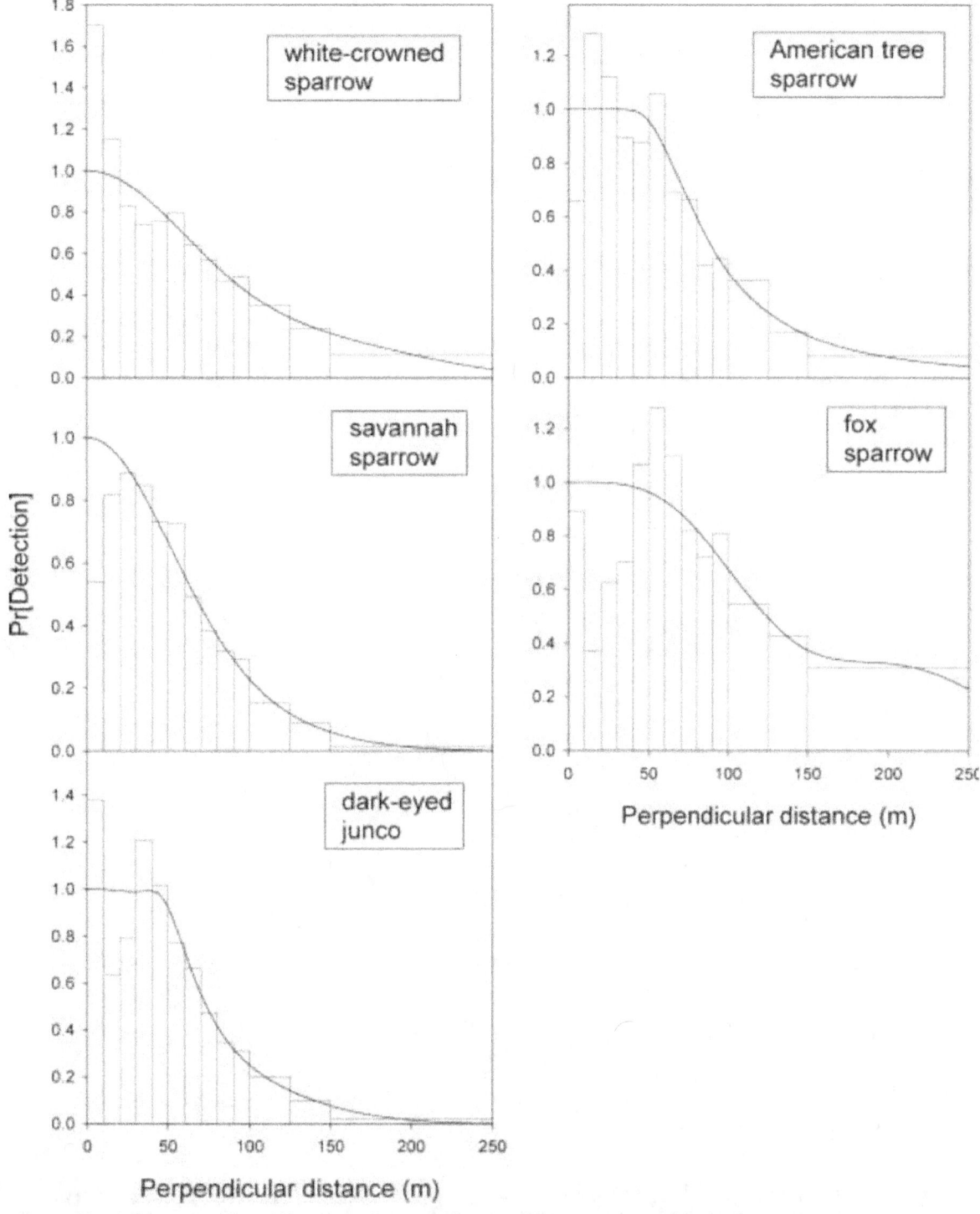

Figure 6a. Estimated detection functions and scaled frequencies of detections for sparrows and allies from point transects in Denali, 2002-2008. Detection function estimated using exact distances and right-truncated at 250 m. Figure continued on next page.

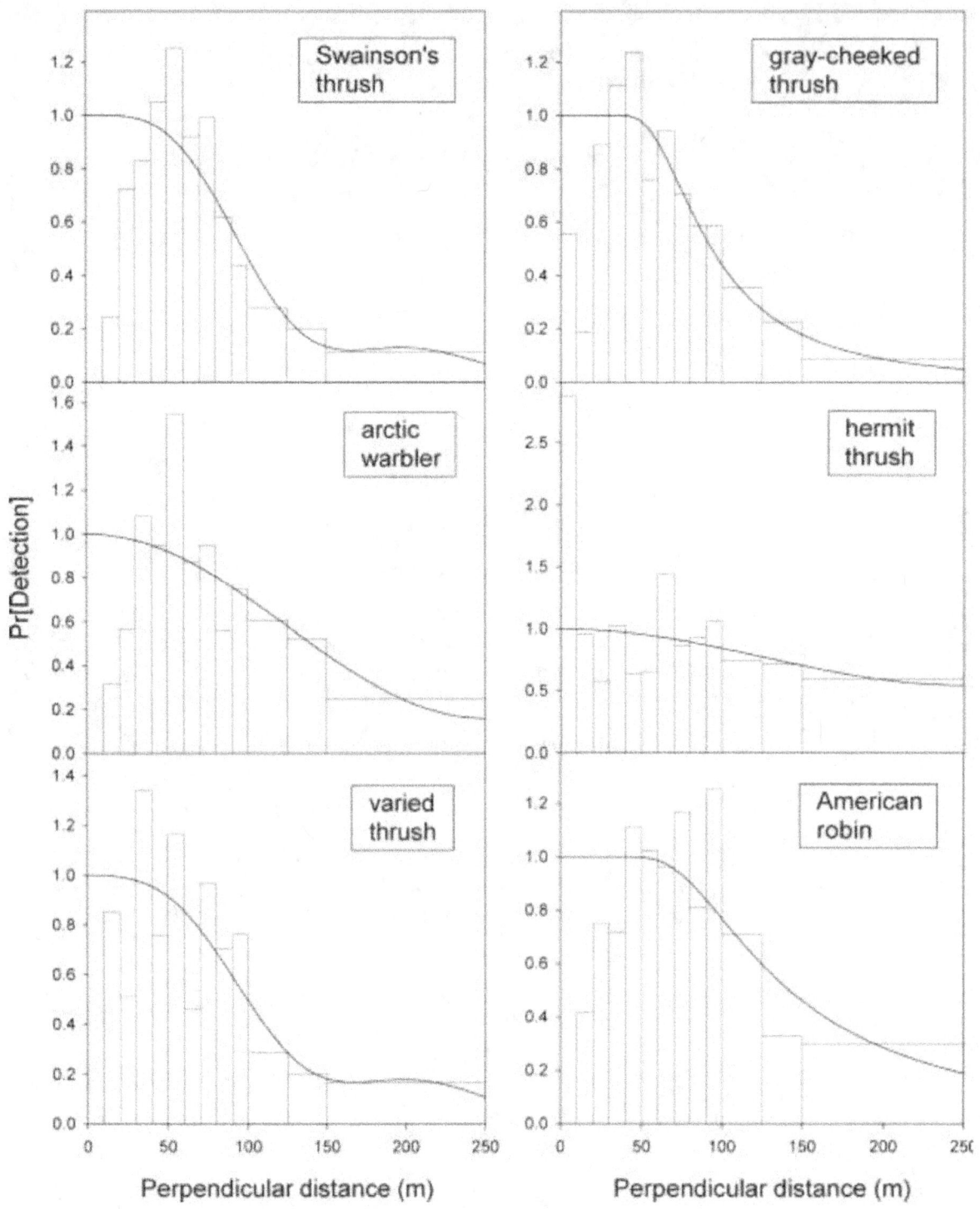

Figure 6b (continued). Estimated detection functions and scaled frequencies of detections for thrushes and arctic warblers from point transects in Denali, 2002-2008. Detection function estimated using exact distances and right-truncated at 250 m. Figure continued on next page.

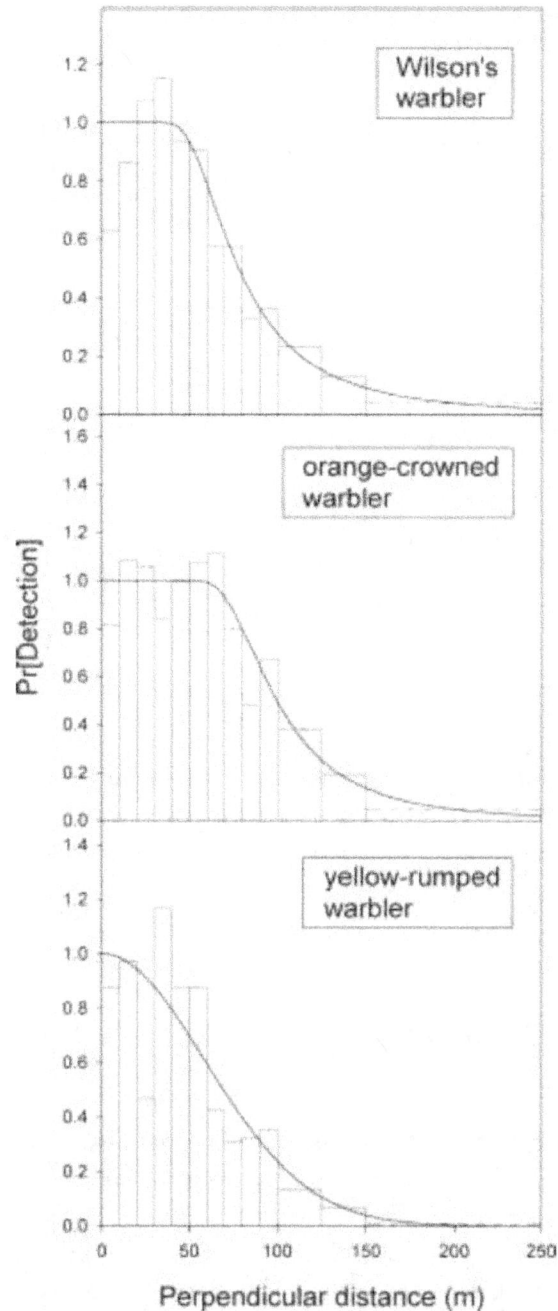

Figure 6c (continued). Estimated detection functions and scaled frequencies of detections for warblers from point transects in Denali, 2002-2008. Detection function estimated using exact distances and right-truncated at 250 m.

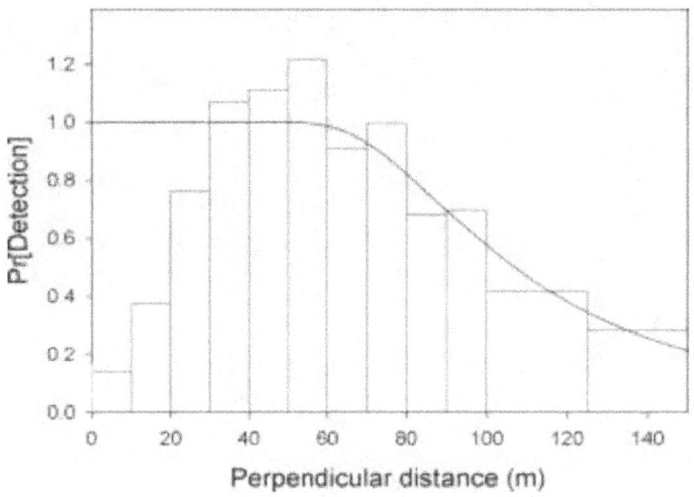

Figure 7. Estimated detection function and scaled frequencies of detections for all thrushes pooled, excepting hermit thrushes, from point transects in Denali, 2002-2008. Detection function estimated using exact distances and right-truncated at 150 m.

Estimated detection functions and scaled frequencies for data pooled across years (Fig. 8) adequately met for these 6 species. For yellow-rumped warblers, the AIC_c-selected detection function (half-normal with a cosine series expansion and 2 adjustment terms) did not meet shape criteria, so we limited candidate models to a single adjustment term. Grouped distance intervals improved the "shoulder" of the detection function for most species, although the shoulder remained relatively narrow for white-crowned and American tree sparrows.

Influence of Covariates on Detection

Modeling effects of year

We limited analyses of covariate effects to 5 species with ≥580 observations to achieve adequate samples within factor levels. Model selection results supported large differences in detection functions among years (Table 5); models pooling years received no credible support. Factor covariate models received overwhelming support in 4 of 5 species. Estimated detection functions varied drastically in scale and shape among years and species (Fig. 9). Differences in shape reflected wide variation in functional form; among species for which factorial models were selected, an average of 5.5 of the 7 detection functions had different combinations of key function plus series expansion. In addition, 17 of the 29 estimated functions had ≥1 series expansion adjustment term(s), often resulting in functions that were not monotonically declining, that had large peaks in detection probability away from the transect center, and that had multiple local peaks. About half of detection functions failed to adequately meet shape criteria.

20

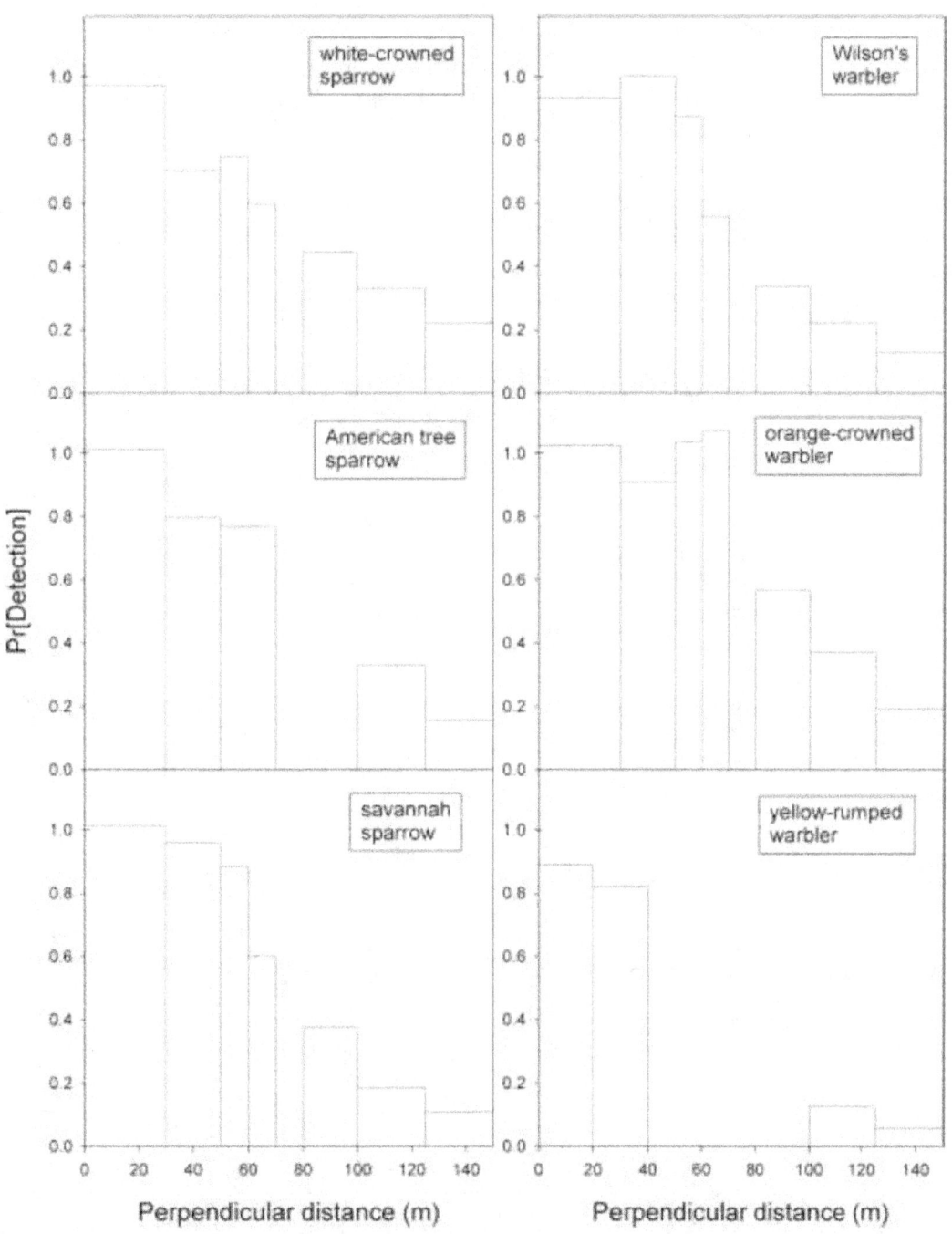

Figure 8. Estimated detection functions and scaled frequencies of detections from point transects for 6 passerines in Denali, 2002-2008. Detections have been right-truncated and grouped to help meet assumptions of distance sampling analyses.

Given problems meeting shape criteria using factor covariate models, we hypothesized covariate models might meet shape criteria while providing adequate goodness-of-fit. The scale covariate model selected for Wilson's warblers produced a consistent and plausible shape for detection functions across years, but substantive differences in shape of the detection function and estimated detection probability relative to the pooled model were cause for concern. In addition, scaled frequencies showed pronounced spikes in detections at 0-30 m in some years and 30-50 m in others, resulting in poor goodness-of-fit of the model to these data (Fig. 10). Similarly, scaled covariate models for other species exhibited poor goodness-of-fit, especially near 0 distance. For example, scaled frequencies for white-crowned sparrows contrasted strongly among years (Fig. 11), with pronounced spikes at 0-30 m or 50-60 m, no appreciable decline from 0-150 m, or uniformly high and low frequencies from 0-70 m and 70-150 m.

Table 5. Selection results for models of effects of year on detection functions. For each species, we considered models pooled across years (no differences between years), with year as a scale covariate (detection functions differed in scale but not shape), and with year as a factor covariate (detection functions differed in scale and shape).

Species	Model	ΔAIC_c[a]	K[b]	AIC_c weight[c]
American tree sparrow	Factor covariate	0.00	16	1.00
	Scale covariate	19.74	7	0.00
	Pooled	40.25	1	0.00
Savannah sparrow	Factor covariate	0.00	16	1.00
	Scale covariate	21.15	8	0.00
	Pooled	42.59	2	0.00
White-crowned sparrow	Factor covariate	0.00	15	1.00
	Scale covariate	25.01	8	0.00
	Pooled	72.22	3	0.00
Orange-crowned warbler	Factor covariate	0.00	14	1.00
	Scale covariate	15.85	8	0.00
	Pooled	19.91	2	0.00
Wilson's warbler	Scale covariate	0.00	8	0.93
	Factor covariate	5.11	15	0.07
	Pooled	12.26	2	0.00

[a]Difference in AIC_c between this and the top model.
[b]Number of estimated parameters.
[c]Weight of evidence as the best approximating model.
[d]Model failed to optimize.

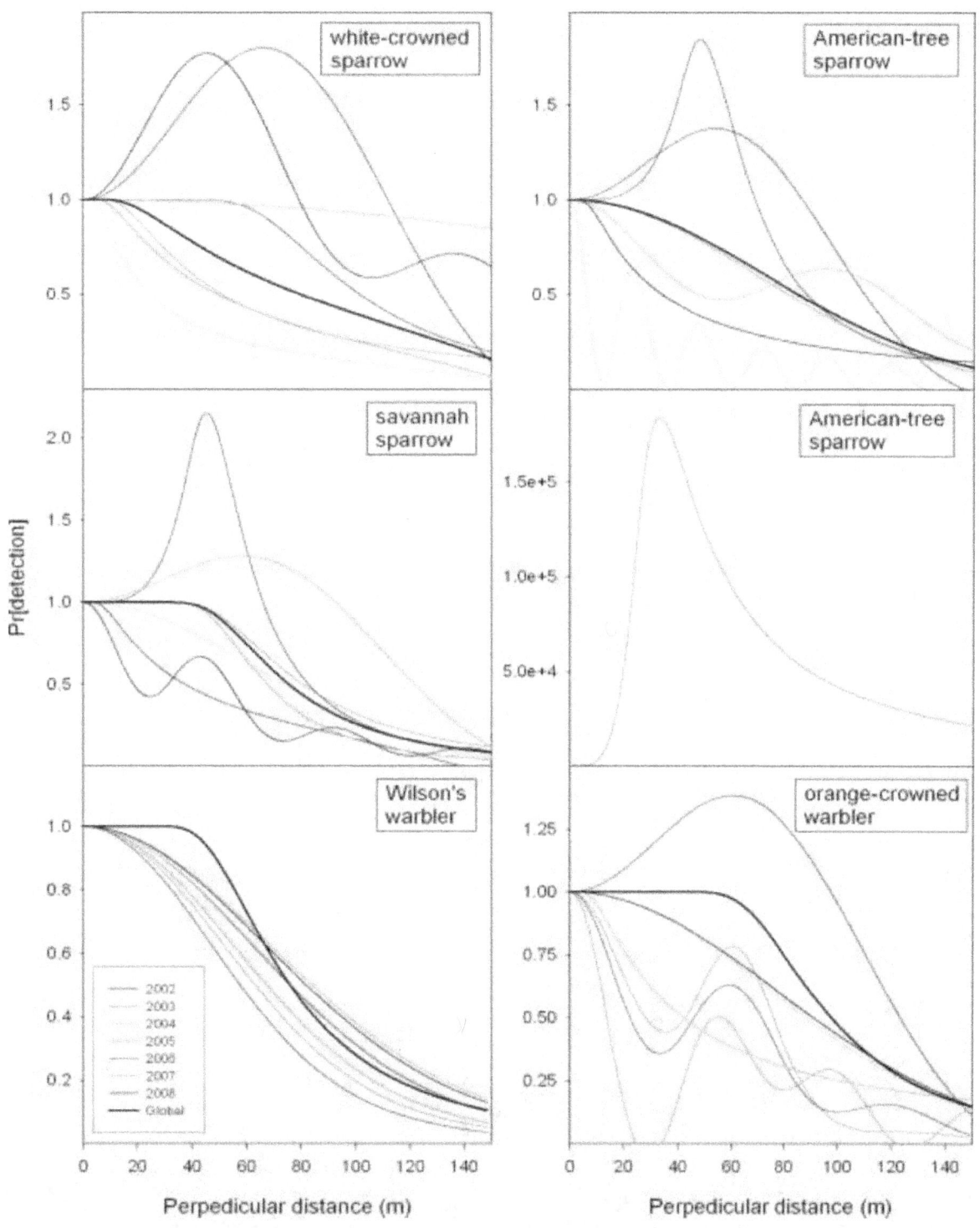

Figure 9. Estimated detection functions for the global model (years pooled) and from the best approximating models describing effects of year from point transects for 5 passerines at Denali, 2002-2008.

23

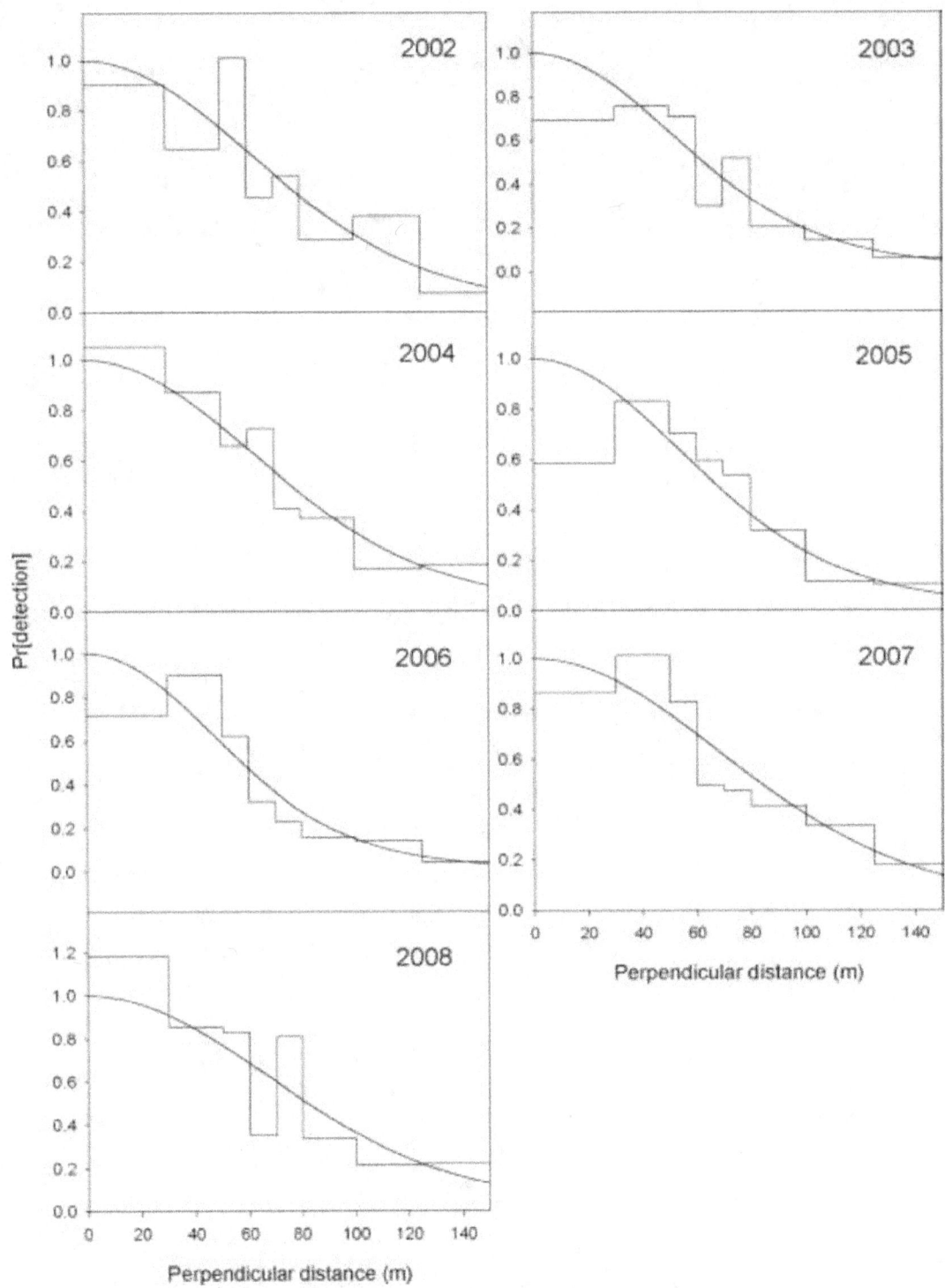

Figure 10. Scaled frequencies of observations (straight lines) and estimated detection functions (curves) by year for Wilson's warblers from point transects in Denali, 2002-2008. Detection functions were estimated from a scale covariate model assuming years differed in scale but not shape.

24

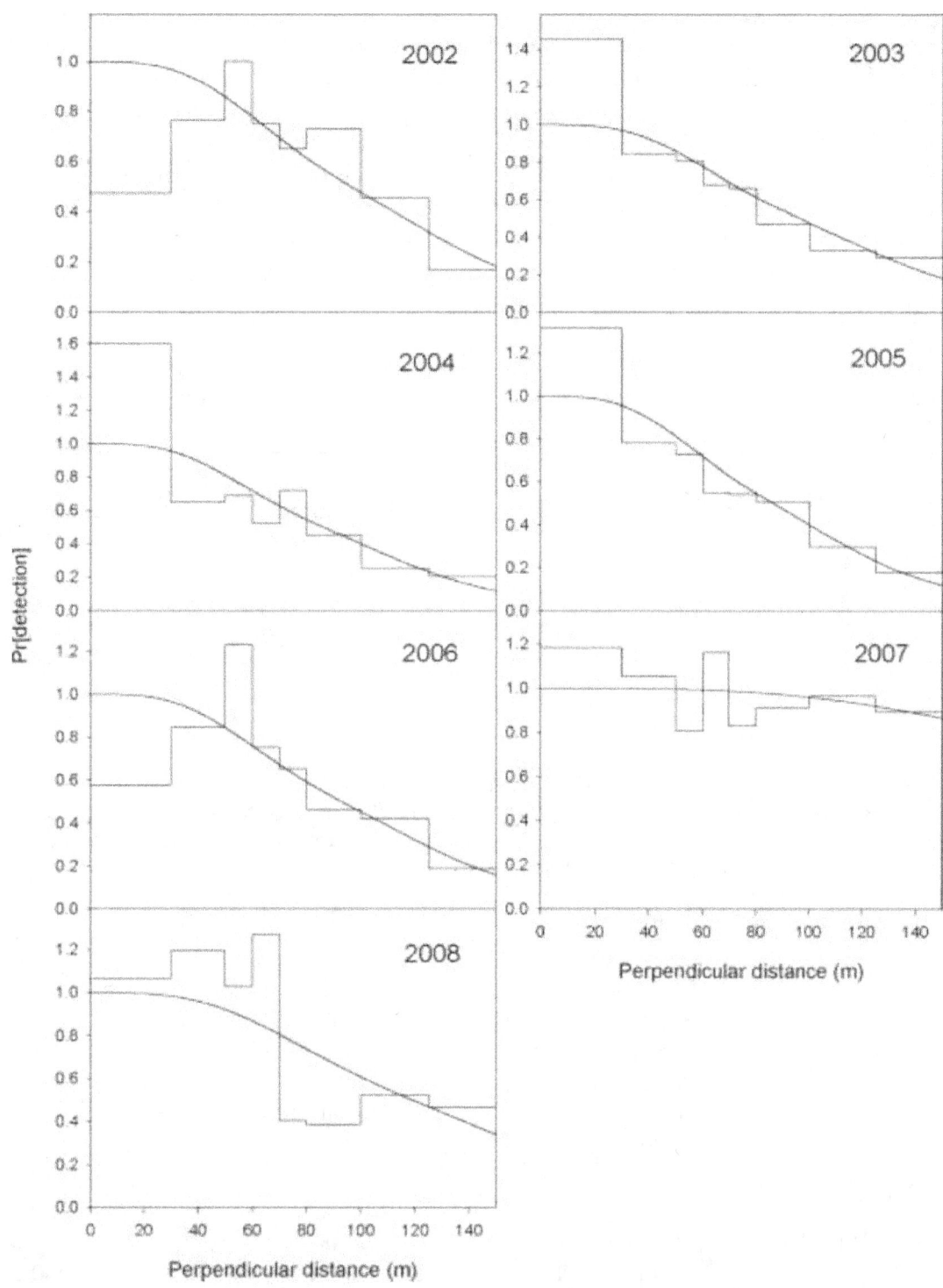

Figure 11. Scaled frequencies of observations (straight lines) and estimated detection functions by year for white-crowned sparrows from point transects in Denali, 2002-2008. Detection functions were estimated from a scale covariate model assuming detection functions differed in scale but not shape.

Modeling effects of observers

The 3 individuals used in our analyses accounted for most observations during 2002-2005 and 20%, 12%, and 13% of all observations (Table 6). We found overwhelming evidence for influence of observers on detection functions (Table 7), with factor covariate models receiving most support. Most detection functions were biologically plausible (Fig. 12), with moderate variation in function shape among observers. Individual observers showed unique tendencies, which were most apparent when viewing scaled frequencies (Fig. 13). Observer 1 showed a high frequency of observations at 0-50 m and then a steep decline. Observer 2 showed a strong peak in observations at 40-60 m, which created severe problems with goodness-of-fit. A gradual, linear decline in observations characterized observer 3.

Table 6. Numbers of observations by 6 individual observers and all other observers during point transects in Denali, 2002-2008.

| | Year | | | | | | |
Group	2002	2003	2004	2005	2006	2007	2008
Other	529	665	154	895	664	11	1094
Observer 1	296	438	790	974			
Observer 2	258	356		913	154		
Observer 3	241		702	759	895		
Observer 4							
Observer 5						936	
Observer 6						899	

Table 7. Selection results for models of effects of select observers on detection functions. For each species, we considered models pooled across observers (no differences between years), with observer as a scale covariate (detection functions differed in scale but not shape), and with observer as a factor covariate (detection functions differed in scale and shape).

Species	Model	ΔAIC_c[a]	K[b]	AIC_c weight[c]
American tree sparrow	Factor covariate	0.00	9	1.00
	Scale covariate	17.82	4	0.00
	Pooled	24.52	1	0.00
Savannah sparrow	Factor covariate	0.00	7	1.00
	Scale covariate	18.90	4	0.00
	Pooled	57.74	2	0.00
White-crowned sparrow	Scale covariate	0.00	7	0.99
	Factor covariate	10.00	7	0.01
	Pooled	77.71	3	0.00
Orange-crowned warbler	Scale covariate	0.00	5	0.61
	Factor covariate	0.90	7	0.39
	Pooled	14.33	2	0.00
Wilson's warbler	Factor covariate	0.00	7	0.94
	Scale covariate	5.40	5	0.06
	Pooled	20.13	2	0.00

[a]Difference in AIC_c between this and the top model.
[b]Number of estimated parameters.
[c]Weight of evidence as the best approximating model.

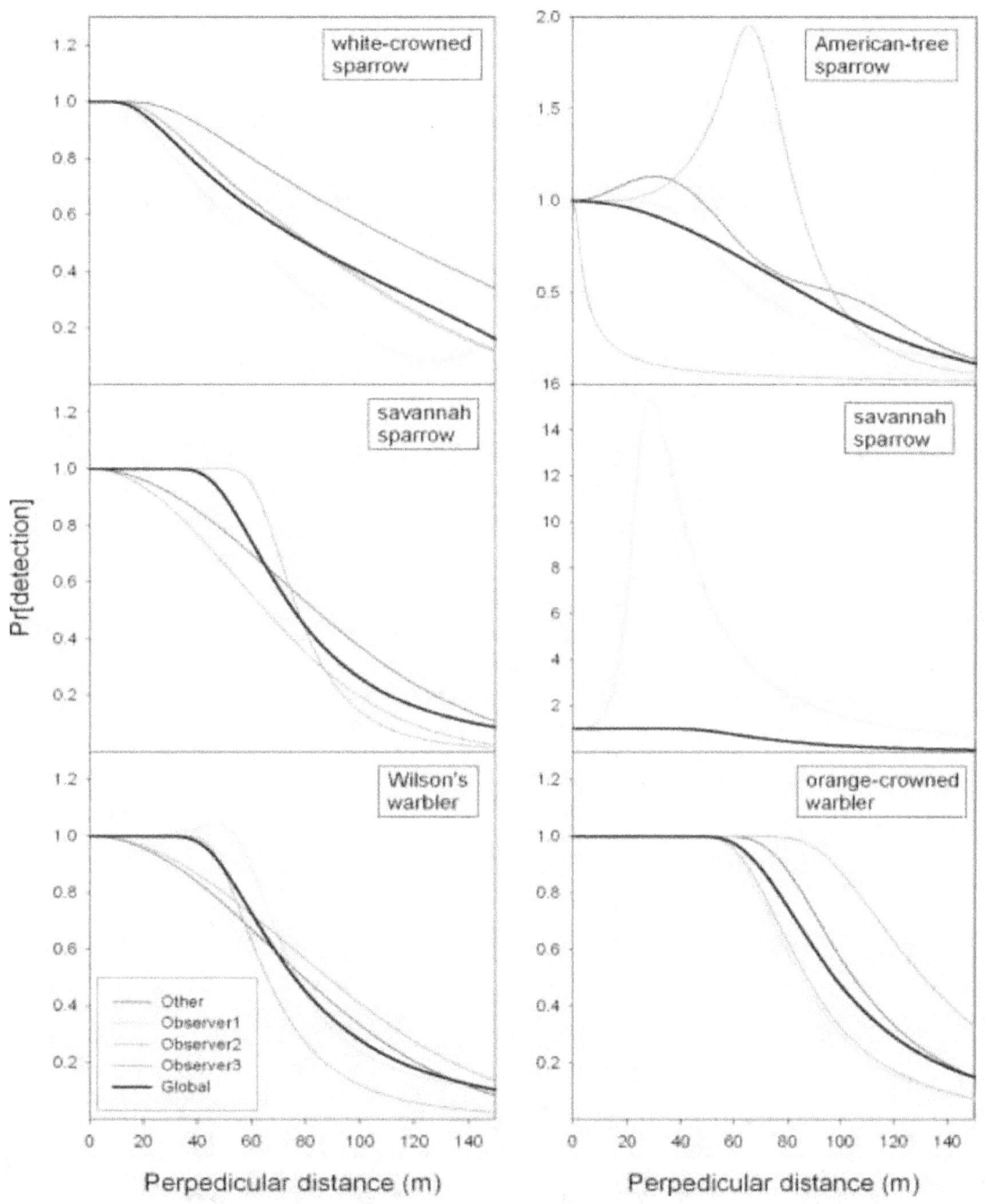

Figure 12. Estimated detection functions for the global model (observers pooled) and from the best approximating models describing effects of observers from point transects in Denali, 2002-2008. Three observers were analyzed individually; remaining observers were pooled in the "other" category.

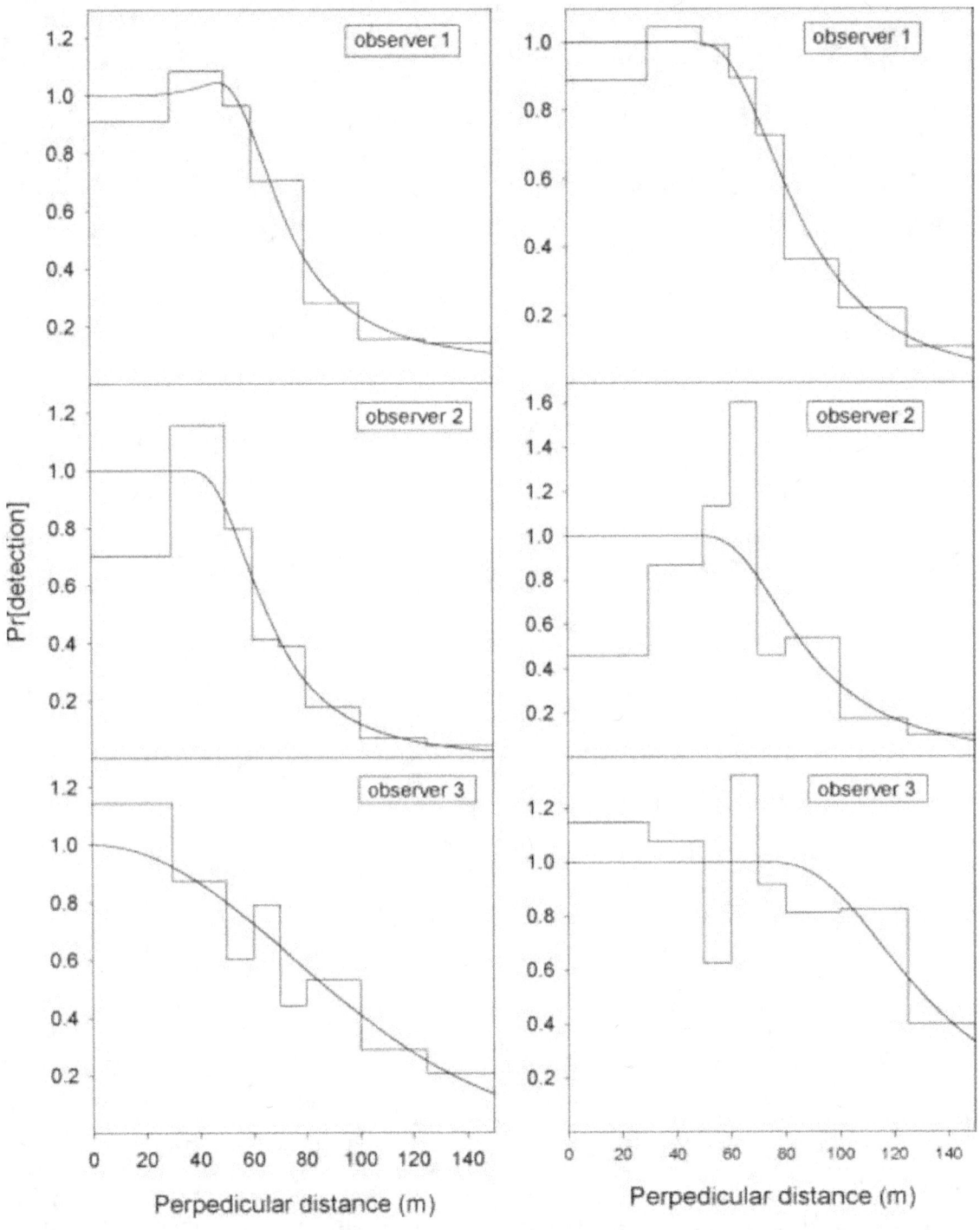

Figure 13. Estimated detection functions and scaled frequencies of observations for 3 unique observers during point transects in Denali, 2002-2008. The left and right column shows results for Wilson's warblers versus orange-crowned warblers.

28

The null hypothesis of omnibus test that proportions of observations by distance interval did not differ for individuals versus all observers was rejected for 5 of 6 observers (df=7 in all cases): observer 1 (χ^2=48.2, P<<0.0001, n=1220); observer 2 (χ^2=56.7, P<<0.00001, n=677); observer 3 (χ^2=10.7, P =0.12, n=708); observer 4 (χ^2=24.0, P =0.002, n=423); observer 5 (χ^2=18.8, 0.006, n=388); observer 6 (χ^2=75.4, P<<0.00001, n=401). Deviations from predicted values show individual patterns for each observer (Fig. 14). Observer 1 and observer 2 had surpluses of observations at small and intermediate distances, with deficits at large distances. In contrast, observer 3 showed an abundance of detections at long distances. A pattern of steadily increasing relative use of distance intervals at larger distance distinguished observers 5 and 6. Observer 4 was unique in conforming to patterns for pooled observers.

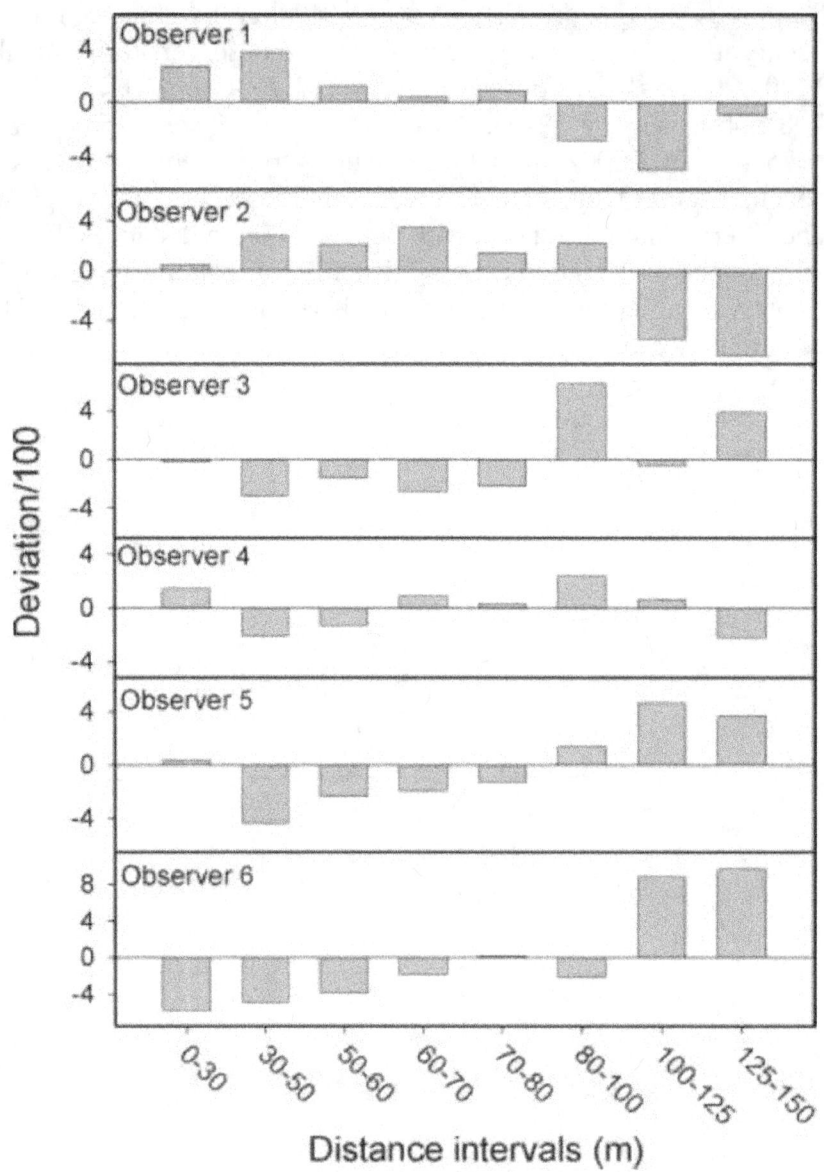

Figure 14. Deviations in detections by distance relative to predicted counts for 6 observers during point transects for passerines in Denali, 2002-2008. Deviations are scaled to show differences in counts per 100 detections.

Modeling effects of habitat

Sampled grids were dominated by scrub habitat (Table 2). Open habitat, which was mostly dwarf scrub, covered almost half the sampled area, and low scrub accounted for another third. Forest habitat, primarily tall scrub and needle leaf forest, accounted for the remaining 22%. Individual grids showed large variation in habitat composition (Table 8), although most were dominated (>75% coverage) by one habitat. Model selection results provided evidence for effects of habitats on detection functions for 4 of 5 species (Table 9): factor and scaled covariate models were selected for 2 species each. For species supporting habitat differences (Fig. 15), most estimated detection functions were biologically plausible and differences in function shapes were moderate. However, estimates did not match the prediction that more open habitats would have higher detection probabilities. An example of scaled frequencies across species and habitats (Fig. 16) demonstrated distributions often violated assumptions and poor goodness-of-fit was common. In addition, effects of habitats were inconsistent across species, as both open and forest habitats showed 3 strongly contrasting patterns: a strong spike in frequencies at small or at intermediate distances or relatively even frequencies over short and intermediate distances with a sharp drop in observations at larger distances.

Table 8. Habitat composition at point transects for passerines in Denali, 2002-2008.

Sampling location	% Open	% Low Scrub	% Forest
Birch Bend	74		26
Cabin Creek	36	36	27
Divide Mountain	100		
Double Mountain	94		6
East Chitsia Mountain			100
EFE	100		
East Fork Toklat River		88	12
Fish Creek	4	44	52
Gorge Creek	100		
Hult Creek	30		70
Igloo Creek	48	32	20
Lower Stony Creek	8	80	12
Lower Thorofare River	76	20	4
Lower East Fork Toklat River	52	48	
MCCN (Moose Creek Canyon)		100	
MCNF (Moose Creek N. Fork)	64	36	
Middle Birch	100		
Middle Fork Teklanika River		44	56
Mount Healy	96		4
Muddy River	95		5
Muldrow	100		
N ka Ridge	56	24	20
Polychrome Pass	44	48	8
Primrose Ridge	96		4
Reinhill	25	75	
Rock Creek	28	4	68
Sanctuary		100	
Tributary Creek	12	71	17
Toklat West	92	8	
Upper Moose Creek		44	56
Upper Savage River	56	32	12
Upper Stony Creek	20	80	
Upper Widgand Creek		84	16
West Fork Toklat River		60	40
Wonder Lake	5	10	85

Table 9. Selection results for models of effects of habitat on detection functions. For each species, we considered models pooled across habitats (no differences between habitats), with habitat as a scale covariate (detection functions differed in scale but not shape), and with habitat as a factor covariate (detection functions differed in scale and shape).

Species	Model	ΔAIC_c[a]	K[b]	AIC_c weight[c]
American tree sparrow	Factor covariate	0.00	7	1.00
	Scale covariate	12.90	3	0.00
	Pooled	17.26	1	0.00
Savannah sparrow	Pooled	0.00	2	0.51
	Scale covariate	1.42	4	0.25
	Factor covariate	1.44	5	0.25
White-crowned sparrow	Factor covariate	0.00	6	0.84
	Scale covariate	3.37	5	0.16
	Pooled	12.97	1	0.00
Orange-crowned warbler	Scale covariate	0.00	4	0.72
	Factor covariate	2.14	5	0.25
	Pooled	6.44	2	0.03
Wilson's warbler	Scale covariate	0.00	5	0.81
	Factor covariate	2.90	4	0.19
	Pooled	37.12	2	0.00

[a]Difference in AIC_c between this and the top model.
[b]Number of estimated parameters.
[c]Weight of evidence as the best approximating model.

White-crowned sparrow (*Zonotrichia leucophrys*).
Photo credit: Donna Dewhurst/USFWS

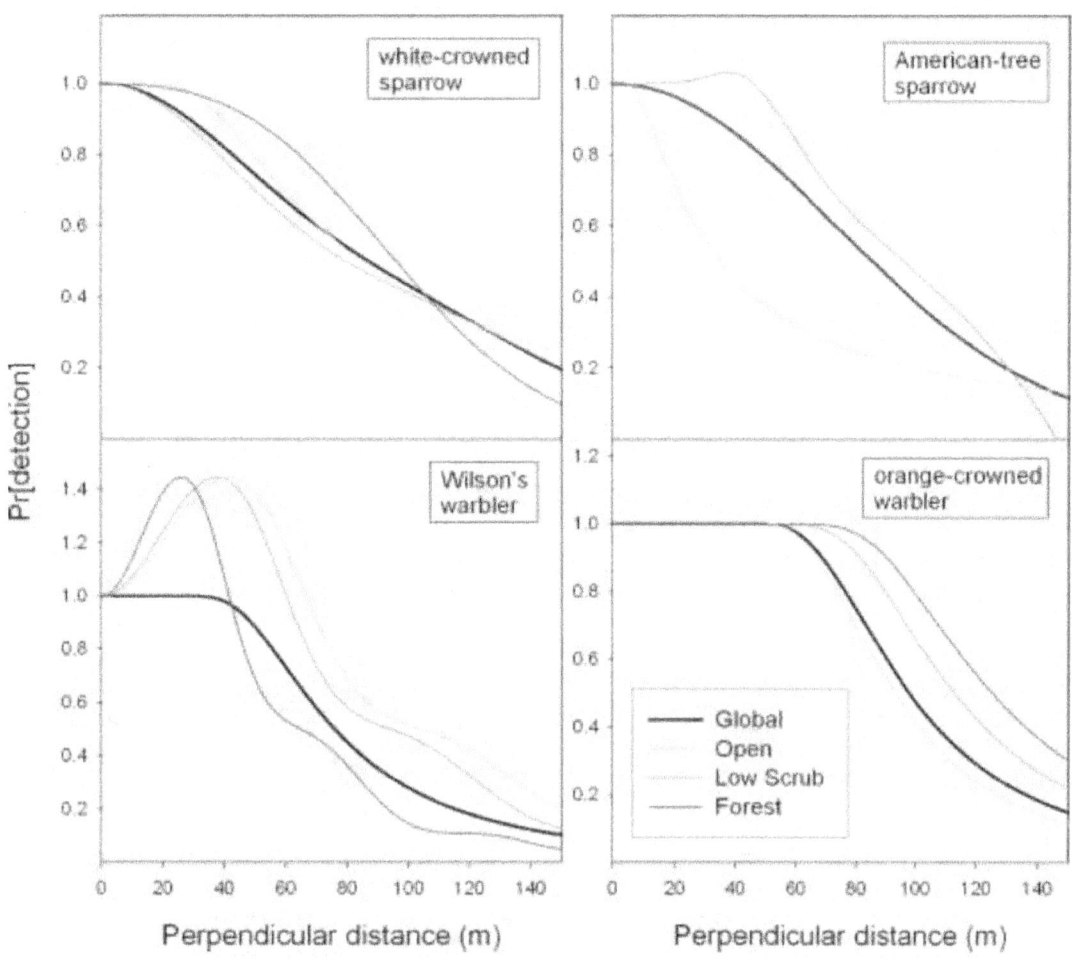

Figure 15. Estimated detection functions for the global model (habitats pooled) and from the best approximating models describing effects of habitat from point transects in Denali, 2002-2008. Results for savannah sparrows are not displayed because effects of habitat were unsupported.

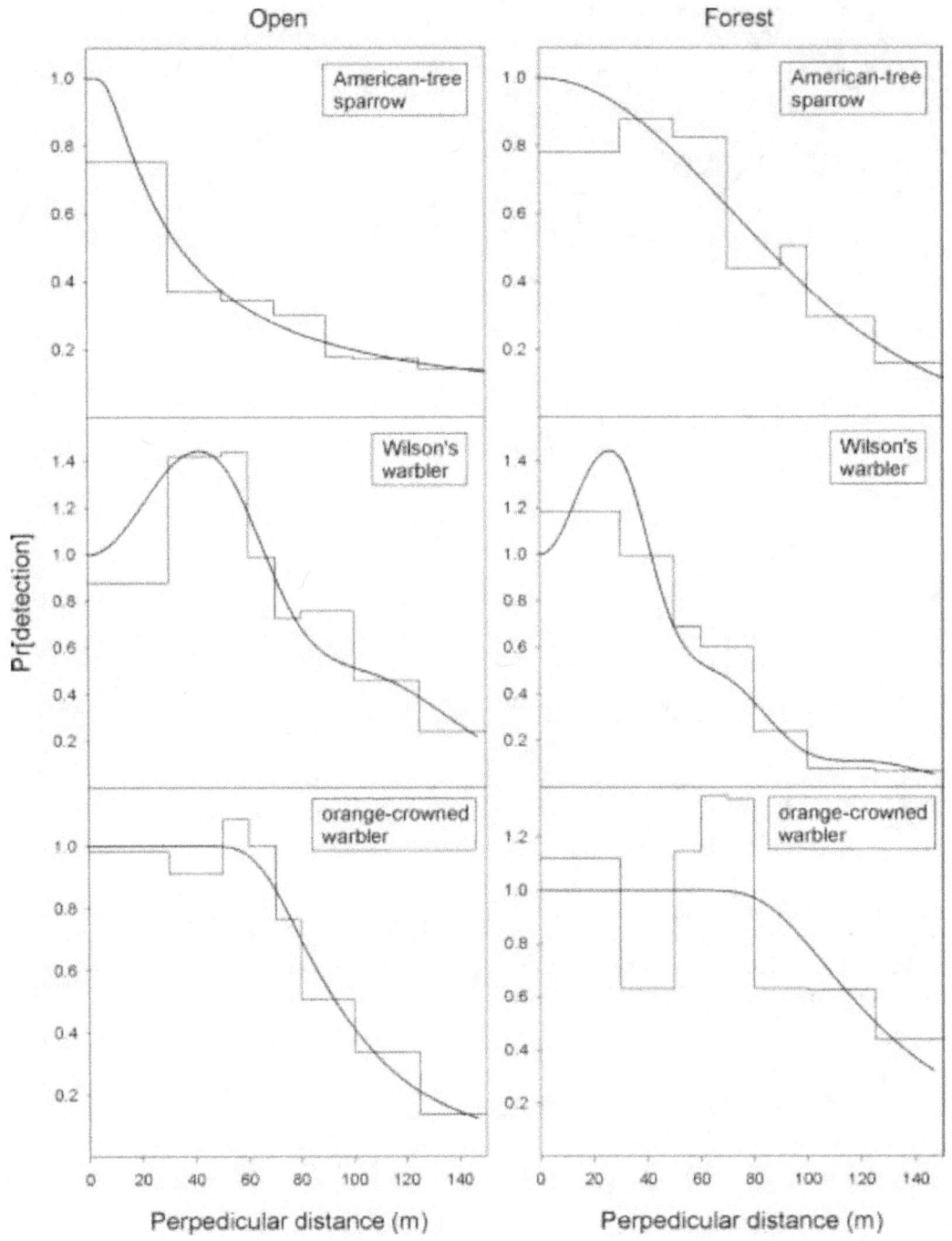

Figure 16. Estimated detection functions and scaled frequencies of detections for 3 passerines during point transects in Denali, 2002-2008. The left and right column shows results for open versus forest habitat.

34

Modeling effects of wind speed

Wind speed was categorized as low for >50% of observations, with the remainder split between moderate and high (Table 1). The estimated correlation between wind speed and habitat type ($r = -0.23$) suggested higher wind in more open habitats but was too weak to raise concerns regarding confounding of these covariates. For all species except Wilson's warbler, model selection results supported effects of wind speed on detection functions (Table 10), with factor covariates models receiving most support. Estimated detection functions followed a relatively consistent pattern that can best be visualized using scaled frequencies (Fig. 17). At low wind speeds, frequencies typically peaked at 0-30 m. In contrast, peaks occurred at 30-80 m at high wind speed, and patterns were intermediate at moderate wind speed. Strong peaks at intermediate distances violated shape criteria and created goodness-of-fit problems. Contrary to predictions, estimates of detection probability increased strongly with wind speed and were on average >2x for high relative to low wind speed.

Table 10. Selection results for models of effects of wind speed on detection functions. For each species, we considered models pooled across wind speeds (no differences between wind speeds), with wind speed as a scale covariate (detection functions differed in scale but not shape), and with wind speed as a factor covariate (detection functions differed in scale and shape).

Species	Model	ΔAIC_c[a]	K[b]	AIC_c weight[c]
American tree sparrow	Factor covariate	0.00	7	0.94
	Scale covariate	5.46	3	0.06
	Pooled	22.59	1	0.00
Savannah sparrow	Factor covariate	0.00	7	0.95
	Scale covariate	6.73	4	0.03
	Pooled	7.80	2	0.02
White-crowned sparrow	Factor covariate	0.00	5	0.77
	Scale covariate	2.43	5	0.23
	Pooled	16.19	2	0.00
Orange-crowned warbler	Factor covariate	0.00	4	0.52
	Scale covariate	0.29	4	0.45
	Pooled	5.59	2	0.03
Wilson's warbler	Pooled	0.00	2	0.56
	Scale covariate	1.66	4	0.24
	Factor covariate	2.05	6	0.20

[a]Difference in AIC_c between this and the top model.
[b]Number of estimated parameters.
[c]Weight of evidence as the best approximating model.

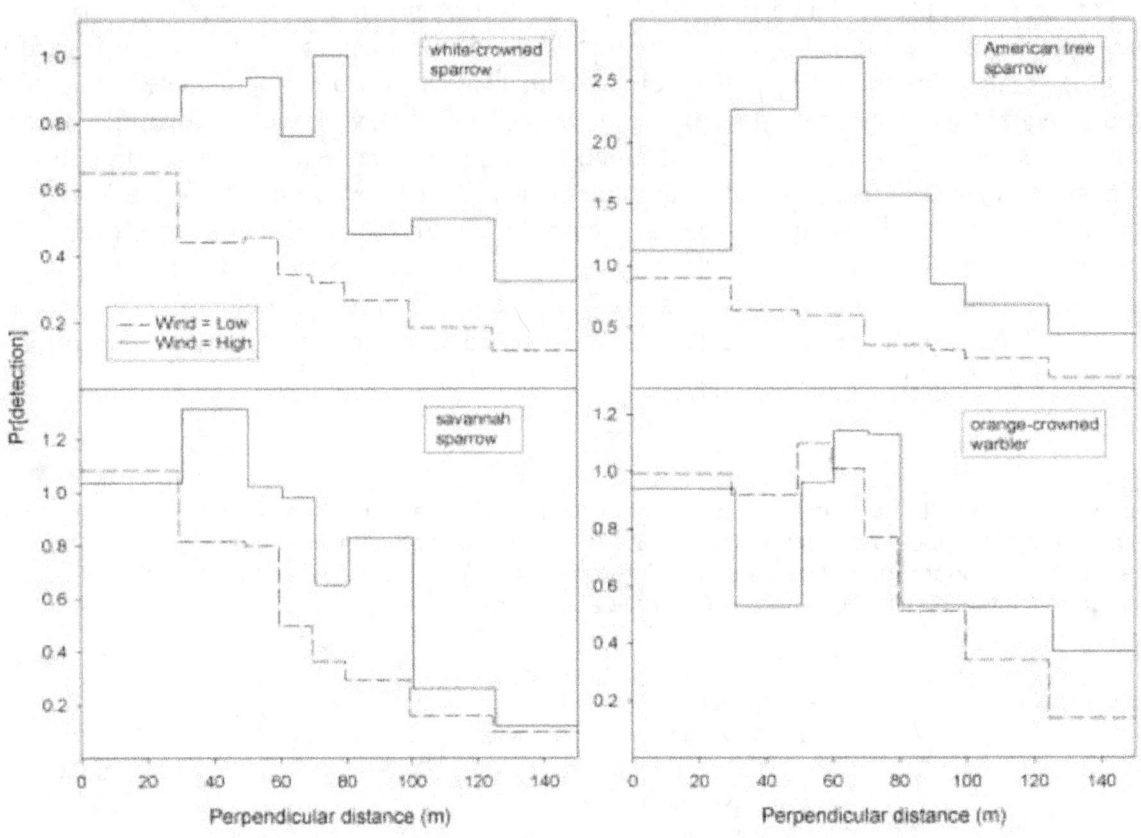

Figure 17. Scaled frequencies of detections for 4 passerines relative to low and high wind speed from point transects in Denali, 2002-2008.

Discussion

Exploratory Analyses

Detection processes varied among species, which had large implications for analyses. Data for many species deviated substantially from assumptions of distance sampling analyses. Resulting complications appeared insurmountable for some species, although palliative measures produced satisfactory results for others. Two prominent problems were surpluses of observations near 0 distance or at intermediate distances.

Elevated frequencies of observations near 0 distance were unlikely to have resulted from detection of birds flushing to evade observers, as most detections were purely aural, or from errors in distance estimation, as trained observers have shown little bias in estimates at short distances (Alldredge et al. 2007b). We also felt it was implausible that sharp declines in detection over short distances resulted from attenuation of loud vocalizations, as experimental results suggest detection probability remains high for many species at <50 m (Alldredge et al. 2007a). Alternatively, increased detection probability near observers might have resulted from disturbance creating increased vocalization rates or movement toward observers. Spikes in detections near 0 distance violate the shape criteria of a flat "shoulder" for the detection function, which is problematic because different key functions provide similar fit to these data but assume different functional forms and hence produce divergent estimates (e.g., Buckland et al. 2001:44-47). Grouping observations at small distances is a remedy we applied that helped flatten the "shoulder" of detection functions. Our preference for the half-normal and hazard key functions, which tend to fit flattened shoulders despite spiked data, was consistent with the assumption that moderate spikes in scaled frequencies result from movement rather than from abrupt changes in detection probability (Buckland et al. 2001). However, surpluses in observations near 0 distance will inevitably create uncertainty in estimation of detection probability.

The strong peaks in scaled frequencies at intermediate distances shared by most thrushes and arctic warblers were similar patterns observed for thrushes elsewhere in Alaska (USGS, Colleen Handel, personal communication, 22 Sep 2008); however, peaks in scaled frequencies were more pronounced and at greater distances in our data. Such peaks could have resulted from hiding or evasive movement of birds near 0 distance. The large size of many thrushes and anecdotal observations of thrushes flushing when approached by observers suggest the latter explanation was more plausible. Circumstantial evidence of errors in distance estimation (see below) suggests an alternative hypothesis. Alldredge et al. (Alldredge et al. 2007b) found observers tended to give similar distance estimates to all aural detections >65 m. Given loud vocalizations of thrushes, probability of detection at long distances likely was high and observers may have perceived these long distance detections to be at intermediate distances. Large unknown bias in distance estimates would preclude reliable estimation of detection functions, but evasive movement might be alleviated by grouping observation distances into larger intervals to create a suitable "shoulder." This approach requires most birds evading from near 0 distance are detected within the first 2 grouped distance intervals. However, large peaks in scaled frequencies at 40-100 m from the transect center for thrushes (Fig. 7) indicated evasive movements often were of sufficient magnitude that probability of detection was almost certainly well <1 for many evading birds. Failure to detect evading birds would also reduce peaks in scaled frequencies at intermediate distances, so patterns likely under-represented distance and frequency of evasive movement. The large ratio (much >1/3) of the distance of apparent evasive movements to average detection distance also reinforces that the magnitude of evasive movement was too large to be remedied by grouping (Buckland et al. 2001). Altering field methods would appear to be the only adequate solution. Gathering suitable data would require either detecting birds at initial locations or approaching transects without causing birds to evade or hide. However, observers attempted to detect evading birds when approaching transects, but with little success. In addition, dense foliage, rugged terrain, and difficulty in locating transects make sufficient improvement in methods unlikely.

Influence of Covariates on Detection Functions

We found strong evidence of large annual variation in estimated detection functions. Wide variation in selected key functions and series expansions produced congruous variation in functional forms, often producing functions that were biologically implausible or violated shape criteria. In such cases, selecting detection functions that met shape criteria provided only cosmetic benefits, as the poor distribution of underlying data resulted in poor goodness-of-fit of models. Imprecision associated with insufficient samples likely did not drive this variation; the average sample for each species and year (162) and the average minimum sample for each species in any year (86) both appeared sufficient relative to the recommended minimum of 75-100 (Buckland et al. 2001). Detection functions that failed to meet shape criteria would not be expected to produce reliable estimates of detection probability or density. Even among models with plausible forms, variation in detection probability appeared unrealistic: as an example, estimates for white-crowned sparrows from 2003-2007 were 0.31, 0.17, 0.28, 0.54, and 0.92. Because detection probability is in the denominator of the density estimator (eq. 2, below), identical encounter rates in 2004 as in 2007 would yield a 541% increase in estimated density, which strained credulity. Annual variability might arise from factors that differed among years, such as habitats at sampled grids, observers, or environmental conditions. However, we discerned no consistent patterns when looking across species within years, and we have no plausible hypothesis to explain large annual variation in the detection process.

Variation in probability of detection among observers has been common for point counts or point transects targeting passerines, and failure to account for differences can produce biased estimates of density or trend (Diefenbach et al. 2003, Sauer et al. 1994). For 3 observers for which we compared detection functions, each showed a unique characteristics that generally were consistent across species. Unlike results for pooled observers or the "other" grouping of 20 observers with smaller samples, detection functions for individuals frequently violated shape criteria or had poor goodness-of-fit. Our interpretation was that pooling observers tended to "average-out" individual heterogeneity and produce more homogenized results. The magnitude of variation in estimates of P_a was much less among observers than years, as P_a among observers within species typically differed by <50% and rarely by >200%. Using a bird song simulation system, Alldredge et al. (2007a) found similar variation among observers.

Omnibus tests also supported individual differences in the detection process. Despite differences in detection functions among species, observers exhibited consistent surpluses or deficits of observations by distance interval relative to pooled observers, suggesting that traits inherent to observers explained differences. As is typical of point transects for passerines in dense vegetation (Brewster and Simons 2009), most detections in this study relied on aural cues. Differences among observers could have resulted from differences in hearing (Emlen and DeJong 1992) or proficiency in identification (Sauer et al. 1994). Alldredge et al. (2007a) concluded these factors drove individual differences in detection and noted that lower overall detection resulted from steeper declines in detection relative to distance. However, this explanation does not address our observation of individual differences in peaks of scaled frequencies (Fig. 13).

Error in distance estimation could also have contributed to individual variation. In an experiment using song playback, Alldredge et al. (2007b) found that bias and error in distance estimates could be large, the relationship between estimated and true distances was non-linear, observers were poor in judging distances >65 m, and training observers produced limited improvements. Error in distance estimation likely is magnified under variable field conditions. A strongly non-linear relationship between true and estimated distances that was unique to each observer would be consistent with large individual differences in distributions of scaled frequencies, as gaps and peaks in distributions would correspond to where a regression of true on estimated distances was "steep" or "flat" (i.e., slope >1 or ~0). We suspect error and bias in distance estimation was problematic in this study. Alldredge et al. (2007b) concluded substantial bias in density estimates could result from both random error and bias in distance estimates.

Habitat can strongly influence probability of detection for passerines (Schieck 1997, Pacifici et al. 2008). Generally, increasing horizontal vegetation density is thought to decrease detection by attenuating vocalizations and increasing ambient noise from leaves in wind; however, interactions between species, environmental conditions, vegetation structure, and detection have been complex (Schieck 1997, Simons et al. 2007, Pacifici et al. 2008). Our sampling locations tended to be dominated by 1 habitat type, but locations varied between relatively open and closed vegetation canopies. We predicted detection probability would decline as canopy closure increased, but effects of habitat were inconsistent and not supported for all species. Estimated detection functions including habitat effects often also exhibited poor-goodness-of-fit to these data.

Decreased detection probability at longer distances with increased wind speed have been attributed to increased ambient noise from moving vegetation (Simons et al. 2007, Pacifici et al. 2008). In contrast, we found increased wind speed consistently elevated scaled frequencies of observations at intermediate distances, which generally increased estimates of P_a. High frequencies of detections at intermediate distances could have resulted from evasive movement by birds or failure to detect birds at short distances, but we felt it implausible that increased wind speed would augment these problems. A more plausible hypothesis was that increased ambient noise exacerbated error in distance estimation by attenuating aural cues and fostering perception that nearby detections were distant.

In sum, our goals of estimating detection probabilities and factors influencing it were impeded by violations of assumptions of distance sampling and large heterogeneity in detection functions. Several recent experimental and field studies have suggested distance sampling methods work well for passerines when assumptions are met, but that assumptions may be difficult to meet in field conditions and have rarely been tested (Alldredge et al. 2007b, Bachler and Liechti 2007, Efford and Dawson 2009, Gale et al. 2009, Nichols et al. 2009, Simons et al. 2009). Violations of assumptions in our data most likely arose from evasive behavior of birds and error in estimating distances from aural cues, and we concluded estimates of detection probability and density suffered from substantial but unknown error and bias. Additionally, extreme heterogeneity in detection functions as well as incomplete detection near 0 distance both undermined the assumed "pooling robustness" of distance sampling (Buckland et al. 2001:389-392), suggesting bias even for estimates from pooled data. We concluded that for our study system overcoming problems associated with distance sampling methods, either through changes to field or analytic methods, likely would be difficult or impossible.

Savannah sparrow (*Passerculus sandwichensis*). Photo credit: Donna Dewhurst/USFWS

Section II: Power to Detect Population Change

Exploratory analyses suggested violations of assumptions of distance sampling introduced substantial error and bias to estimates. Therefore, we adapted goals and methods for this section. We dropped from further analyses species with behaviors that appeared incompatible with distance sampling. For 6 remaining species, we felt presenting estimates of detection probability and density was inappropriate. However, we were still interested in assessing power because the magnitude of bias was unknown and because bias in density estimates alone would not invalidate estimates of population trend if there were no temporal trend in bias. To assess whether the methods and sampling effort in this pilot study could potentially meet monitoring objectives, our approach was to examine a "best-case scenario" that minimized effects of bias.

The monitoring objective was to achieve 80% statistical power to detect a 50% population decline over 20 years for multiple species (McIntyre et al. 2004), where statistical power is the probability of detecting a statistically significant decline given that such a decline exists (Thompson et al. 1998). Power to detect population trend is strongly inversely related to temporal variation in population estimates (Larsen et al. 2001). However, detection functions that strongly deviated from shape criteria produced implausibly large annual variation among estimates of detection probability and hence density, which would depress estimates of power. To minimize variation arising from estimation problems and produce reasonable estimates of annual variation in density, we used statistical criteria and judgment to select detection functions meeting shape criteria. For each species, we estimated power to detect a decline of 50% over 20 years, as well as less severe declines of 35% and 20% over 20 years (annual declines of 3.4%, 2.2%, and 1.1%).

Additional to total variation in density estimates, the structure of variation also influences power to detect trends (Larsen et al. 2001). Annual variation may be divided into 2 components: coherent variation (consistent across sites) and interaction variation (site-specific variation). Coherent variation is especially problematic for trend detection because associated reduction in power is relatively insensitive to sampling design or spatial replication. Because variation in encounter rates in this and other studies has dominated total variation in density estimates (Buckland et al. 2001) we simplified estimation of coherent variation by using encounter rates as a surrogate to density.

Methods

Estimating Annual Variation in Density

Estimating power to detect annual trend in density requires reliable estimation of the standard error of estimation S.E.$_{est}$, defined as annual variation in density estimates around the trend (Hatch 2003). We estimated density using distance sampling theory (Buckland et al. 2001). Density is a function of the encounter rate E (detections/transect), the size S of each group (1 or more individuals in close proximity) detected, and the probability P_a of detecting groups within the surveyed area. We estimated P_a as

$$P_a = \frac{\int_0^w g(x)\,dx}{w}, \tag{1}$$

where $g(x)$ is the estimated detection function and w is the right-truncation distance. We estimated density D as

$$D = \frac{E \cdot S}{2 \cdot w \cdot P_a}, \tag{2}$$

where S was the average group size. We estimated variance in encounter rates using the design-derived estimator for random sampling designs, denoted R2 in Program DISTANCE v. 6 and Fewster et al. (2009).

Because we found large annual variation in detection probabilities, obtaining independent estimates of density across years required separate annual estimates of detection probability. We selected best approximating detection functions using AIC$_c$ (as described above in *Exploratory Analyses*), except when resulting functions violated shape criteria. In such cases, we reduced the number of series expansion terms to 1 or 0 until we judged that the AIC$_c$-selected model met shape criteria. We then used density estimates from selected models to estimate S.E.$_{est}$ using methods of Hatch (2003). Few locations were sampled in multiple years, which is necessary to estimate coherent variation. For this analysis, we selected 7 sites that were sampled in 2005 and 2006 (Table 3). We partitioned between year variance in encounter rates into its components using methods described by Lewis (1978).

Estimating Power to Detect Decline

Power analyses.- We estimated power using Programs TRENDS (Gerrodette 1993), with a type I error rate $\alpha = 0.05$, a 1-sided test for an exponentially declining population, a Coefficient of Variation = S.E.$_{est}$/(average density across all years). Variance of density estimates from point transects typically is dominated by variance in encounters among transects (Buckland et al. 2001). Because variation in encounters can reasonably be described as a Poisson-like process (Fewster et al. 2009), we selected the TRENDS option stipulating that the CV was constant relative to abundance.

Results

Power to Detect Decline

In the process of selecting a set of "best" models for estimating detection functions, we retained the AIC_c-selected top model in only 8 of 40 cases. None of the final models included series expansion terms, resulting in detection functions with very tractable shapes but sometimes with large deviations from the data. For many cases where scaled frequencies showed a spike or deficit in observations near the transect center, we selected the hazard function because it provided a flat "shoulder" in these circumstances. Strong peaks in densities for most species during the middle years of the study contributed to high estimated CV's of annual variation in density.

For the least stringent scenario of detecting a 50% decline in populations over 20 years, 80% power was achieved for savannah sparrows and Wilson's warblers, but would not be achieved for other species until well beyond 20 years (Fig. 18). Power to detect more moderate declines of 35% and 20% over 20 years was low for all species Table 11). For sites sampled in both 2005 and 2006, we estimated coherent variation in encounter rates between years accounted for an average of 36% of the total variation. Furthermore, coherent variation was on average 19% of the mean encounter rate.

Table 11. Estimated power to detect population decline over a twenty year period at three levels of overall population decline. Estimates are for 6 species of passerines in Denali based on data collected during 2002-2008. Estimated CV's were from 7 years, except for yellow-rumped warblers which had insufficient samples for 2 years.

Species	CV[a]	% decline over 20 years		
		-50%	-35%	-20%
White-crowned sparrow	0.62	0.48	0.26	0.13
American tree sparrow	0.51	0.59	0.31	0.15
Savannah sparrow	0.31	0.91	0.58	0.25
Wilson's warbler	0.35	0.85	0.50	0.22
Orange-crowned warbler	0.45	0.68	0.37	0.17
Yellow-rumped warbler	0.55	0.55	0.29	0.09

[a]Coefficient of variation in estimates of density around the population trend (see text for additional detail).

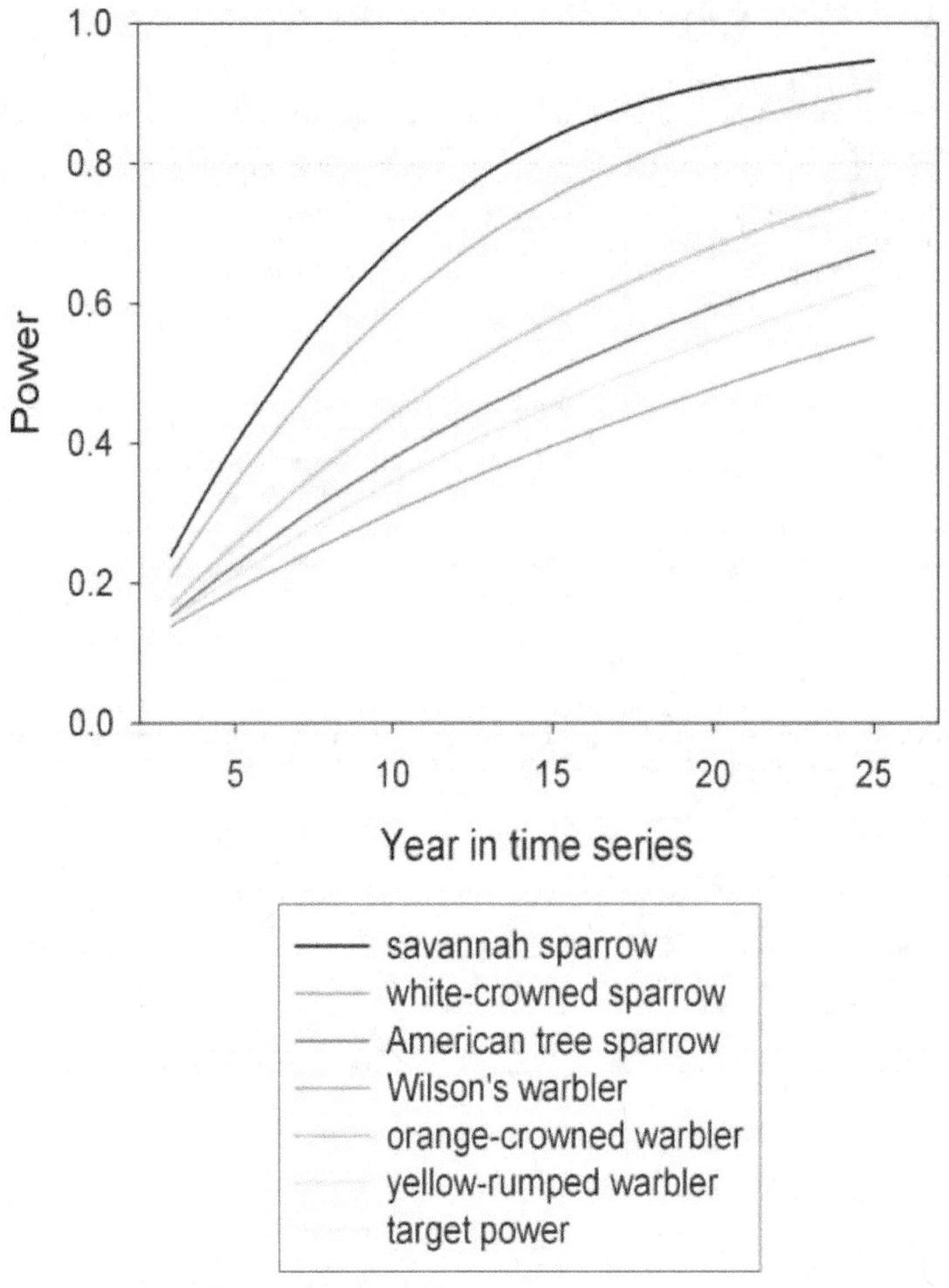

Figure 18. Estimated power to detect a decline in a population declining 50% over 20 years for 6 passerines in Denali. Estimates based on sampling design and data from point transects, 2002-2008.

Discussion

Given the sampling design and sampling effort in Denali during 2002-2008, we concluded the passerine monitoring program would be unlikely to meet its goal of detecting 50% population declines over 20 years for multiple species (McIntyre et al. 2004). Among dozens of species detected, only 14 had sufficient observations for reliable estimation of density. Eight of these showed behaviors that severely violated assumptions of point transect sampling and were suitable for further analyses. Of the remaining 6, estimated power to detect severe declines exceeded specified targets for only 2 species, and power to detect more moderate declines was very low for all species.

Low power resulted from high annual variation in density estimates, which was driven by peaks during the middle years of the study. Annual variation in density estimates combined temporal and spatial variation, because in most years most mini-grids were not surveyed in the previous year. If spatial variation is large relative to temporal variation, then a survey design including a high proportion of repeat visits to sites in different years (e.g., panel designs) can yield a substantial increase in power to detect trends (Urquhart and Kincaid 1999). However, we found that coherent annual variation in encounter rates accounted for 36% of the total variance. Power to detect trend is highly sensitive to coherent variation, and even small amounts can dramatically reduce power. For a passerine monitoring program similar to this one, Powell et al. (2007) estimated 10-15% coherent variation and concluded that increasing coherent variation quickly drove power to detect population decline to unacceptably low levels. Deleterious effects of coherent variation are insensitive to design decisions and typically can be mitigated primarily by increasing the length of the time series (Larsen et al. 2001). Although our estimates should be viewed with caution because they are derived from only 7 sites across 2 years, high estimated coherent variation suggested gains in power to detect trend from designs employing revisits to sites were likely to be modest.

To produce density estimates for power analyses, we used a model selection procedure that favored use of simplified models to estimate detection functions relative to AIC_c-selected models. Resulting detection functions fulfilled shape criteria for distance analyses and avoided extreme and unrealistic density estimates. However, many of these simplified models showed serious problems with goodness-of-fit, and density estimates likely were overly precise and tended toward the overall average for each species. Hence, annual variation among estimates likely was underestimated, and our model selection procedures likely inflated estimates of power to an unknown degree.

Other regional monitoring protocols for passerines employing point transect surveys have used pilot data to assess ability to monitor multiple species. For Olympic National Park, Siegel et al. (2007) examined whether sampling ~240 point transects annually would yield 80% power to detect a 56% decline over 20 years. They projected this goal could be met for 16 species; however, their simulations did not include annual fluctuations in population size, differences in trends among sampling sites, variation in probability of detection among years or observers, or uncertainty or variation in structures of models of detection functions. For the Sonoran Desert National Parks, Powell et al. (2007) examined power to detect declines of 46% over 20 years using a design with 1,162 point transects surveyed annually. They concluded sufficient power might be achieved for ~24 species, depending on levels of annual variation in populations.

Simulations of power assumed no variation in probability of detection among observers or years. Neither study provided information concerning adherence to assumptions or sources of variation in detection. In contrast, our relatively pessimistic assessment of power to detect trend can be attributed to several factors: relatively modest sampling effort (~200 point transects annually), severe violations of assumptions of analyses, large variation in estimated detection probabilities, large annual variation in density estimates, and a strong coherent component to annual variation.

Orange-crowned warbler (*Vermivora celata*). Photo credit: Donna Dewhurst/USFWS

Conclusions and Recommendations

We found strong evidence of severe violations of assumptions of distance sampling methods, likely resulting from behavior of study species and error in distance estimation. We concluded estimates of detection probability and density likely were subject to large error and bias. We also found large variation in the detection process relative to year, habitat, and wind speed. Patterns were often inconsistent with expectations, and we suspect multiple sources of variation in detection interacted to produce observed variation. High heterogeneity in detection functions resulted in similar variation in estimates of detection probability and density, which decreased power to detect population trend. Even with optimistic assumptions, meeting monitoring goals for passerine populations in Denali unlikely if current methods were continued.

These results did not stem from deficiencies in methods, study design, or training and performance. Rather, evasive behaviors by birds and difficulty in estimating distances to auditory detections of birds appeared to be critical problems inherent to the study system that were difficult or impossible to circumvent by altering field or analytic methods. Therefore, point transect surveys appear inappropriate for monitoring passerine populations in Denali. We recommend using methods allowing estimation of detection probabilities but that do not require estimation of distance to detected birds and are robust to evasive movements of birds in response to observers. Potentially suitable approaches include methods employing passive detector arrays, repeated counts at a sampling point, time to detection, and multiple observers (Farnsworth et al. 2002, Wenger and Freeman 2008, Efford et al. 2009, Joseph et al. 2009, Nichols et al. 2009). A drawback is many of these methods estimate only population indices, although monitoring population trend and distributions may feasible. Proposed methods should be carefully evaluated to ensure assumptions of each method and programmatic goals can be met.

Literature Cited

Alldredge, M., T. Simons, and K. Pollock. 2007a. Factors affecting aural detections of songbirds. Ecological Applications 17:948-955.

Alldredge, M., T. Simons, and K. Pollock. 2007b. A field evaluation of distance measurement error in auditory avian point count surveys. Journal of Wildlife Management 71:2759-2766.

Bachler, E., and F. Liechti. 2007. On the importance of g(0) for estimating bird population densities with standard distance-sampling: Implications from a telemetry study and a literature review. Ibis 149:693-700.

Bibby, C. J., N. D. Burgess, D. A. Hill, and S. H. Mustoe. 2007. Bird census techniques, 2nd edition. Academic Press, San Diego, California, USA.

Brewster, J. P., and T. R. Simons. 2009. Testing the importance of auditory detections in avian point counts. Journal of Field Ornithology 80:178-182.

Buckland, S. T., D. R. Anderson, K. P. Burnham, J. L. Laake, D. L. Borchers, and L. Thomas. 2001. Introduction to Distance Sampling: Estimating Abundance of Biological Populations. Oxford University Press, New York, New York, USA.

Buckland, S. T., D. R. Anderson, K. P. Burnham, J. L. Laake, D. L. Borchers, and L. Thomas. 2004. Advanced Distance Sampling: Estimating Abundance of Biological Populations. Oxford University Press, New York, New York, USA.

Burnham, K. P., and D. R. Anderson. 2002. Model Selection and Multi-Model Inference, 2nd edition. Springer, New York, New York, USA.

Diefenbach, D., D. Brauning, and J. Mattice. 2003. Variability in grassland bird counts related to observer differences and species detection rates. Auk 120:1168-1179.

Efford, M., and D. Dawson. 2009. Effect of distance-related heterogeneity on population size estimates from point counts. Auk 126:100-111.

Efford, M., D. Dawson, and D. Borchers. 2009. Population density estimated from locations of individuals on a passive detector array. Ecology 90:2676-2682.

Emlen, J., and M. DeJong. 1992. Counting birds - the problem of variable hearing abilities. Journal of Field Ornithology 63:26-31.

Fancy, S. G., and J. R. Sauer. 2000. Recommended methods for inventorying and monitoring of biological resources in national parks. National Park Service, Ft. Collins, Colorado, USA.

Farnsworth, G., K. Pollock, J. Nichols, T. Simons, J. Hines, and J. Sauer. 2002. A removal model for estimating detection probabilities from point-count surveys. Auk 119:414-425.

Fewster, R., S. Buckland, K. Burnham, D. Borchers, P. Jupp, J. Laake, and L. Thomas. 2009. Estimating the encounter rate variance in distance sampling. Biometrics 65:225-236.

Gale, G. A., P. D. Round, A. J. Pierce, S. Nimnuan, A. Pattanavibool, and W. Y. Brockelman. 2009. A field test of distance sampling methods for a tropical forest bird community. Auk 126:439-448.

Gerrodette, T. 1993. TRENDS: software for a power analysis of linear regression. Wildlife Society Bulletin 21:515-516.

Hatch, S. A. 2003. Statistical power for detecting trends with applications to seabird monitoring. Biological Conservation 111:317-329.

Johnson, D. H. 2008. In defense of indices: The case of bird surveys. Journal of Wildlife Management 72:857-868.

Joseph, L. N., C. Elkin, T. G. Martin, and H. P. Possingham. 2009. Modeling abundance using N-mixture models: the importance of considering ecological mechanisms. Ecological Applications 19:631-642.

Larsen, D. P., T. M. Kincaid, S. E. Jacobs, and N. S. Urquhart. 2001. Designs for evaluating local and regional scale trends. Bioscience 51:1069-1078.

Lewis, W. M. J. 1978. Comparison of temporal and spatial variation in the zooplankton of a lake by means of variance components. Ecology 59:666-671.

Link, W. A., and J. R. Sauer. 1998. Estimating population change from count data: Application to the North American Breeding Bird Survey. Ecological Applications 8:258-268.

MacCluskie, M., and K. Oakley. 2005. Vital Signs Monitoring Plan, Central Alaska Network, Vital Signs Monitoring Plan. U.S. Department of Interior, National Park Service, Fairbanks, Alaska.

McIntyre, C. L., R. Drum, K. Oakley, E. Debevec, T. McDonald, and N. Guldager. 2004. Passerine bird monitoring protocol for the Central Alaska Monitoring Network: Denali National Park and Preserve, Wrangel-St. Elias National Park and Preserve, and Yukon-Charley Rivers National Preserve, Alaska. U.S. Department of the Interior, Unpublished Report, Fairbanks, Alaska, USA.

Nichols, J. D., L. Thomas, and P. B. Conn. 2009. Inferences about landbird abundance from count data: Recent advances and future directions. Pages 201-235 in D. L. Thompson, E. G. Cooch, and M. J. Conroy, editors. Modeling Demographic Processes in Marked Populations. Springer, New York, New York, USA.

Norvell, R. E., F. P. Howe, and J. R. Parrish. 2003. A seven-year comparison of relative-abundance and distance-sampling methods. Auk 120:1013-1028.

Nowacki, G., P. Spencer, M. Fleming, T. Brock, and T. Jorgenson. 2002. Unified ecoregions of Alaska. U.S. Geological Survey Open File Report 02-297.

O'Connell, T. J., L. E. Jackson, and R. P. Brooks. 2000. Bird guilds as indicators of ecological condition in the central Appalachians. Ecological Applications 10:1706-1721.

Pacifici, K., T. Simons, and K. Pollock. 2008. Effects of vegetation and background noise on the detection process in auditory avian point-count surveys. Auk 125:600-607.

Paton, P. W. C., and T. H. Pogson. 1996. Relative abundance, migration strategy, and habitat use of birds breeding in Denali National Park, Alaska. Canadian Field-Naturalist 110:599-606.

Peterjohn, B. G. 1994. The North American Breeding Bird Survey. Birding 26:386-398.

Powell, B. F., A. D. Flesch, D. Angell, K. Beaupre, and W. L. Halvorson. 2007. Landbird monitoring protocol for the Sonoran Desert Network. Version 1.02. National Park Service, Fort Collins, Colorado, USA.

Ralph, C. J., S. Droege, and J. R. Sauer. 1995. Managing and monitoring birds using point counts: Standards and applications. Pages 161–168 in C. J. Ralph, J. R. Sauer, and S. Droege, editors. Monitoring Bird Populations by Point Counts. U.S. Department of Agriculture, U. S. Forest Service General Technical Report PSW-GTR-149.

Robbins, C. S. 1981. Effect of time of day on bird activity. Studies in Avian Biology 6:275-286.

Roland, C., K. Oakley, and C. McInytre. 2003. Evaluation of a study design for detecting ecological change in Denali National Park and Preserve at multiple scales. Long-term ecological monitoring program, Denali National Park and Preserve, and USGS-Alaska Science Center. 2 volumes.

Rosenstock, S., D. Anderson, K. Giesen, T. Leukering, and M. Carter. 2002. Landbird counting techniques: Current practices and an alternative. Auk 119:46-53.

Sauer, J. R., J. E. Fallon, and R. Johnson. 2003. Use of North American Breeding Bird Survey data to estimate population change for bird conservation regions. Journal of Wildlife Management 67:372-389.

Sauer, J., B. Peterjohn, and W. Link. 1994. Observer differences in the north-American breeding bird survey. Auk 111:50-62.

Schieck, J. 1997. Biased detection of bird vocalizations affects comparisons of bird abundance among forested habitats. Condor 99:179-190.

Siegel, R. B., R. L. Wilkerson, K. J. Jenkins, R. C. Kuntz II, J. R. Boetsch, J. P. Schaberl, and P. J. Happe. 2007. Landbird monitoring protocol for national parks in the North Coast and Cascades Network. U.S. Geological Survey Techniques and Methods 2–A6, Reston, Virginia, USA

Simons, T. R., K. H. Pollock, J. M. Wettroth, M. W. Alldredge, K. Pacifici, and J. Brewster. 2009. Sources of measurement error, misclassification error, and bias in auditory avian point count data. Pages 237-254 *in* D. L. Thompson, E. G. Cooch, and M. J. Conroy, editors. Modeling Demographic Processes in Marked Populations. Springer, New York, New York, USA.

Simons, T., M. Alldredge, K. Pollock, and J. Wettroth. 2007. Experimental analysis of the auditory detection process on avian point counts. Auk 124:986-999.

Skirvin, A. A. 1981. Effect of time of day and time of season on the number of observations and density estimates of breeding birds. Studies in Avian Biology 6:271-274.

Thomas, L., J. L. Laake, E. Rexstad, S. Strindberg, F. F. C. Marques, S. T. Buckland, D. L. Borchers, D. R. Anderson, K. P. Burnham, M. L. Burt, S. L. Hedley, J. H. Pollard, J. R. B. Bishop, and T. A. Marques. 2009. Distance 6.0. Release 2. Research Unit for Wildlife Population Assessment, University of St. Andrews, UK. Available at http://www.ruwpa.st-and.ac.uk/distance/ (accessed 14 Feb 2011).

Thomas, L., S. T. Buckland, E. A. Rexstad, J. L. Laake, S. Strindberg, S. L. Hedley, J. R. Bishop, T. A. Marques, and K. P. Burnham. 2010. Distance software: Design and analysis of distance sampling surveys for estimating population size. Journal of Applied Ecology 47:5-14.

Thompson, W. L., G. C. White, and C. Gowan. 1998. Monitoring Vertebrate Populations. Academic Press, San Diego, California, USA.

Urquhart, N. S., and T. M. Kincaid. 1999. Designs for detecting trend from repeated surveys of ecological resources. Journal of Agricultural Biological and Environmental Statistics 4:404-414.

Viereck, L. A., C. T. Dyrness, A. R. Batten, and K. J. Wenzlick. 1992. The Alaska vegetation classification. U.S. Department of Agriculture, Forest Service, Pacific Northwest Research Station. Portland, Oregon, USA.

Wenger, S. J., and M. C. Freeman. 2008. Estimating species occurrence, abundance, and detection probability using zero-inflated distributions. Ecology 89:2953-2959.

NPS 184/114759, June 2012